Building and Leading
New Academic Programs
in Higher Education

Building and Leading New Academic Programs in Higher Education

A Practical Guide for Faculty

Gretchen Oltman and Jackie Clark

ROWMAN & LITTLEFIELD
Lanham • Boulder • New York • London

Rowman & Littlefield
Bloomsbury Publishing Inc, 1385 Broadway, New York, NY 10018, USA
Bloomsbury Publishing Plc, 50 Bedford Square, London, WC1B 3DP, UK
Bloomsbury Publishing Ireland, 29 Earlsfort Terrace, Dublin 2, D02 AY28, Ireland
www.rowman.com

Copyright © 2025 by Gretchen Oltman and Jackie Clark

All rights reserved. No part of this publication may be: i) reproduced or transmitted in any form, electronic or mechanical, including photocopying, recording or by means of any information storage or retrieval system without prior permission in writing from the publishers; or ii) used or reproduced in any way for the training, development or operation of artificial intelligence (AI) technologies, including generative AI technologies. The rights holders expressly reserve this publication from the text and data mining exception as per Article 4(3) of the Digital Single Market Directive (EU) 2019/790.

British Library Cataloguing in Publication information available

Library of Congress Cataloging-in-Publication Data available

ISBN 978-1-4758-6603-2 (cloth)
ISBN 978-1-4758-6604-9 (pbk.)
ISBN 978-1-4758-6605-6 (ebook)

For product safety related questions contact productsafety@bloomsbury.com.

Contents

PART I: BUILDING NEW ACADEMIC PROGRAMS IN HIGHER EDUCATION   1

1	The Launch	3
	Why Now?	4
	Why You?	5
	The Benefits to the Institution	5
	The Benefits to the Faculty	6
	The Benefits to the Student	7
	The Guiding Question for Faculty	8
	Understanding the Place of the Program: Why This New Program at This Institution at This Time?	9
	Standing in the Middle of Chaos	11
	A Leading and Learning Adventure	14
	The Challenge of Self-Doubt	15
	How to Use This Book	15
	The Purpose of Reflection and How We Will Guide This Process in This Book	17
	Questions for Your Reflection	17
2	New Academic Proposals	19
	The Necessity for Proper Planning	20
	A Universal Framework	20
	Components of a Typical Proposal	21
	Comprehensive Proposal Elements	30
	Section 1: Program Description	31
	Section 2: Rationale for the Program (Need and Justification)	32
	Section 3: Evidence of Need for the Program	33

Section 4: Potential Costs of a New Program	34
Section 5: Similar and Related Programs	36
Section 6: Preparation for Ongoing Education	37
Section 7: Quality and Other Aspects of the Program	38
Section 8: Anticipated Student Enrollment	40
Questions for Your Reflection	40

3 Political Maneuverings and Persuasive Language (Internal and External Stakeholders, Collaboration, and Political Considerations) — 41

Understanding the "Academic Capitalist Regime"	42
The Market-Driven Culture of Academia	43
Mission, Vision, and Strategic Planning: Building on Existing Foundations	44
What Does This All Mean When Developing a New Academic Program?	46
Barriers to New Program Development: Internal vs. External	46
The Layers	47
The Role of Stakeholders	49
Resistance to Change	51
The High Cost of Innovation	53
Organizational Culture	53
Collaboration as an Essential Development Skill	54
Questions for Your Reflection	55
Suggested Readings	55

4 Organizing for Student Learning — 57

Prioritizing Learning in New Program Development	57
Learning Outcomes Alignment	58
Alignment with Institutional Outcomes	58
Creating Program Outcomes	59
A Formula for Program Outcome Design	61
Crafting Course Learning Outcomes	61
Ensuring Outcomes Encourage Learning	62
Assessment	63
Accreditation	64
Questions for Your Reflection	65

PART II: LEADING NEW ACADEMIC PROGRAMS IN HIGHER EDUCATION — 67

5 Leaning into Leadership — 69

How'd You Get Here Anyway?	69
Leadership 101 for New Academic Program Leaders	70
Figuring Out How You Lead	72

	Leadership Mentors	73
	Failure within Leadership	74
	Prioritizing Self-Care	75
	Questions for Your Reflection	76
6	Leading Students in a New Academic Program	77
	Who Are the Students That We Serve?	78
	Where Do You Find Key Student Demographics Data?	83
	High-Impact Practices	84
	How Do You Use This Information to Lead a New Academic Program?	84
	Questions for Your Reflection	85
7	Preparing to Lead Faculty	87
	The Importance of Faculty	87
	Estimating Faculty Needs within a New Academic Program	89
	Navigating Your Own Faculty Role	90
	Advocating for More Personnel over Time	91
	Part-Time and Full-Time Additions to the Team	92
	Growing Others and Yourself at the Same Time	93
	Sharing Faculty	93
	Questions for Your Reflection	95
8	Reflections about Leading, Building, and Implementation	97
	The Thrill of Leading	97
	The Agony of Leading	98
	Advice to a New Academic Program Leader	99
	Things We Know Now That We Wish We Would've Learned Earlier	100
	Conclusion	102
References		103
Index		107
About the Authors		113

Part I

BUILDING NEW ACADEMIC PROGRAMS IN HIGHER EDUCATION

Chapter 1

The Launch

Overview: Have you been tapped on the shoulder to start a new academic degree program? Where does an academic professional even start to unpack this new job duty? This chapter helps faculty, who are often untrained in leadership and/or program development, to take a broader look at the task and to begin to answer an essential question: Why this new program at this institution at this time? Academic professionals are illustrated as architects, and a wide overview of the challenges and opportunities of new program development is presented.

One of the best and most challenging aspects of working as an academic professional at an institution of higher education is the ability to innovate and change the landscape of the future of education. Yes, some of us enter the ranks of faculty to spend more time studying our pet research interests or to inspire young scholars, but a faculty career can also provide a path for creativity and thinking outside the box. If you've picked up this book, it is likely that you have been in the same position as so many other faculty in nearly every institution—that is, you've been tapped on the shoulder and asked to start a new academic degree program, start a new major, or tear down and reconstruct an existing academic program. Over the course of the past decade, as the competition for students has increased and the financial strain on institutions has magnified, new academic programs are an easy way to reinvent a tired and maybe even outdated curriculum.

For our purposes in this book, we call this process a "launch." Much like building a rocket from the ground-up, placing it on a launching pad, sending it into space, watching it evolve and explore, and then eagerly awaiting its return to Earth, so too is this process of building an academic "rocket" from scratch. Granted, it lacks the flame and international appeal, but it is noteworthy in and of itself. For an academic—a faculty member entrenched in an institution of higher education—formulating and building a new major, new program, or even new degree path can be just as complicated.

WHY NOW?

From the outside looking in, it may seem that institutions of higher education, from community colleges to private universities to for-profit educational corporations, are set in their ways—offering the same majors and courses of study to incoming students, all in an effort to meet accreditation standards, the needs of a changing workforce, or the demand for education beyond the K–12 environment. But today's colleges and universities are competing for students—which means educational institutions have become more like competitors than friends. The price of a college education has increased, and many students are bypassing traditional college routes in favor of trade schools or apprentice programs. In return, colleges and universities, in an effort to meet the needs of today's students and to have a competitive edge in recruiting, must adapt and change with the times. In 2018, the Hechinger Report cited federal figures that colleges and universities have increased new programs and majors by 21 percent since 2012—roughly 41,446 degree or certificate programs (Marcus, 2019). Thus, we've seen the emergence of dynamic and interesting new academic programs at institutions around the world all in an attempt to capture today's students.

Adding new majors or academic programs has not resolved the issue of the lack of students enrolling in college today; rather, it has appealed to a different audience—that is, a generation that is seeking skills to use in the workforce and shorter, simpler paths to a degree. Granted, the need for traditional liberal arts education is certainly present—we do subscribe to the idea that studying the liberal arts, like music, drama, philosophy, and other core studies can be a transformational experience for students—teaching them how to think rather than what to think, using challenging academic inquiry processes to study humanity and the state of human affairs both in the past and present. But we cannot ignore that colleges have not expanded liberal arts in this current drive to enroll students—instead, they have proposed new majors (like cybersecurity, e-gaming, and sustainability) and developed course offerings in more accessible formats, like online, asynchronous, or remote settings—meaning a student can access their education from literally anywhere in the world. Higher education, it seems, while more expensive than ever in most places, is also more interesting and innovative than ever before.

WHY YOU?

You picked up this book because you understand the task being investigated—the development and implementation of a new academic program at the post-secondary level. Regardless of where you work, the size or type of your institution, and your rank or discipline, you need to understand and manage this process. You might be thinking about proposing a new certificate program or degree path or you might be an administrator tasked with increasing revenue year after year. Regardless, you know, by picking up this book, that starting a new program is more than generating an idea. It has many, many steps and in almost any institution, it has many layers of convincing, navigating, and maneuvering even to get the first student enrolled. Our investigation and experience in starting new programs (between the two authors, we have at least developed or helped launch four different programs at different degree levels at different types of institutions) have shown us that there is no faculty manual for this process. Thus, we are left scouring institutional policies, asking colleagues at neighboring institutions for guidance, and often faltering and falling along the way. This does not mean that starting a new program is too hard—it is not. As noted previously, institutions are starting new types and levels of programs now more than ever before, but that does not mean there is sufficient guidance for faculty tasked with the everyday work of building the structure behind the program.

THE BENEFITS TO THE INSTITUTION

Offering new approaches to content within choices of majors, degree programs, certificate offerings, or even advanced degree choices offers several benefits to the institution willing to invest in this expansion. First, the competitive edge to engage with potential students is a great selling point. If a college can say, "Only *we* offer this degree in Global Food Studies," it may sway a student to choose that college over another. Additionally, education as a process is meant to change and evolve. That is, while maintaining programs of studies in classic and traditional areas provides a strong base for a traditional undergraduate population, the image a college or university can portray by continuously evolving and embracing new areas of study shows that an institution has not grown stale or set in its ways. Much like we see in consumer product evolutions, brands change, packaging is remade to be flashier and more appealing to the eye, so too can "education" be remade into something that the student desires to have in his or her life.

To be clear, not all change and innovation are viable. Many times, in recent decades, internal and external constituencies have suggested specific changes that were touted as benefits but turned out to be disasters. For example, eliminating graduate programs to "focus" on undergraduate students only, streamlining/eliminating programs due to public pressure, removing faculty autonomy and leadership, and capping or controlling the delicate mix of programs in a college. How could educated and knowledgeable professionals make such critical errors in judgment? David Labaree, Stanford professor and higher education historian, provides an answer in his book *A Perfect Mess*. In his book, he addresses the unique composition and complexity of the higher education system in the United States and how its evolved form is its source of strength. This form is rife with complex structures that coexist in specifically dependent ways; therefore, to tamper with it is to risk disaster. In order for new academic programs to be successful and provide a benefit to the institution, there must be a careful structural examination conducted so as not to disturb this "perfect mess" but rather become a part of the rich and interconnected ecosystem of each individual campus.

The additional revenue seen by a college or university as a result of launching a new program can be anywhere from minimal to astounding, particularly in the area of graduate education, where most new programs are offered. PBS reported in 2018 that many colleges and universities were leveraging their graduate programs as a means of stabilizing their budgets. Because more employers require master's degrees, there has been a massive growth in graduate programs overall with the US Department of Education reporting triple the number of master's degrees conferred between 1970 (236,000) and 2015 (759,000). Graduate degrees, it seems, are not only high in demand but almost necessary for career advancement in today's workforce. Thus, institutions seeking to increase the bottom line of the budget can easily add graduate programs, charge higher tuition, and continue to see a demand for the academic degree.

THE BENEFITS TO THE FACULTY

While there are economic benefits to institutions that offer new programs and access to degrees, there are also some not-so-obvious benefits to the faculty tasked with working in or building a new degree program. Embracing intellectual adventure, faculty are able to begin a content area from scratch, without the confines of the old adage that "it's always been done this way so we must keep doing it this way." Freedom from constraints of faculty expectations, student demands, and administrative red tape, building a new program from the ground up can be exactly what an academic needs—the push to build something new and worthwhile, to invent intellectually, and to be responsible for his or her contribution to the field. Most faculty do not work in higher education for fame and money (some do), but most are student-driven or content-passionate. As a result, having the chance to step onto a campus and be the creator of something yet to be developed can be a career reviver.

In addition, new programs also provide new opportunities for faculty to develop different roles for themselves—from coach to facilitator to investor to leader. Colleges and universities have recently admitted to struggles with the tenure-track guarantees that many faculty earn. While this process can protect academic integrity and freedom for the faculty member, it can also cost the institution more in higher salaries, more selective workloads, and the inability to change faculty roles if necessary (Kafka, 2021). Opening the possibility that faculty roles might be reenvisioned, changed over time, and even shifted to different purposes can provide longevity for a faculty member who may have grown weary or tired of continuing to teach the same course load year after year.

Last, new programs might be a timely response to the intellectual growth within an academic field or discipline. For example, textbooks in biology have tripled in content in the past twenty-five years, so how do faculty reinvent programs that engage students with that new content? It's a direct outgrowth of research and teaching—the focus of faculty work. Reinventing programs or starting new programs is a form of scholarship in its purest sense. Thus, we would be remiss to think the college majors of yesterday must remain intact as they were in order to be relevant to students of today and generations to come.

THE BENEFITS TO THE STUDENT

The workforce of today (and tomorrow) has drastically changed in the past two decades. Even within the current decade, with the 2020 worldwide pandemic that shifted many workers to remote workstations, the need for adaptability, flexibility, and creativity has never been more in demand. However, students are not always the first to recognize or even understand the complexities of new program development—the many layers of approvals, the shifting of dollars, and even the tenuous nature of starting a new academic focus, so they may enroll in a new program without a lot of knowledge of what is going on behind the scenes in academic leadership. Thus, while innovative programming and creative endeavors on the part of the university may be cumbersome and challenging, students can benefit from a university or college that seeks to improve processes and develop opportunities for students to be competitive in the workforce. Granted, not all new degree programs will match with a trendy new job title or position at an up-and-coming start-up company, but students who are able to recognize the work being done to develop a new academic program may also benefit from being part of that building process, from influencing course development and structures to pressing for accountability in outcomes from their coursework. In all, students who partner with faculty in new program development can share the experience as an intellectual and administrative pursuit. This process is part of a larger change movement in response to job shifts, future projections, and workforce development. Schools, in turn, are more responsive and are working to differentiate themselves competitively. These are all strong attributes for students as there are more focused programs, more connection to careers/jobs, and more options that are forward-looking to future careers.

THE GUIDING QUESTION FOR FACULTY

New program development is certainly beneficial to higher education as a whole. It provides benefits for students, faculty, the institution, as well as institutional partners, the community, and the impacted academic field of research and study. But as someone identified to begin or implement a new program, you may be left staring at a blank screen wondering where to start. As an academic, you have most likely always been the driver of your academic pursuits. Your work through graduate school, entering higher education as a teacher or researcher, and serving the university or college has most likely been a pursuit of fitting in and following suit with what was expected of you. The path to promotion, advancement within your field, or finding a place as an academic was probably something you were able to figure out along the way, talking to others in similar positions, learning from your institution, and simply building your academic career.

The new program launch, however, asks faculty to step outside the predictable path to the professorship. It places the responsibility for understanding change, program management, curriculum development, assessment processes, and even bureaucratic red tape on the shoulders of you—someone who probably has very little training in any or all of these areas. Additionally, it pushes you outside your comfort zone into an area full of excitement and challenge. Starting a new program can feel like building a rocket but can also feel like your work on the rocket will never succeed and never be noticed.

Therefore, it can be helpful for faculty approached with or assigned a new program development of any sort to answer one guiding question:

Why this new program at this institution at this time?

That is, it is important for you, the reader, the faculty member who was identified as the candidate to be the driving force behind a new program, major, or academic endeavor, to understand your role in the process. Sure, you may have been selected because you are the most senior faculty in your department or because you happened to be at the right place at the right time for a new academic appointment, but all of that really does not matter. What does matter is how you understand, conceptualize, and manage your role in this process—one that can be exciting, terrifying, and invigorating all at the same time.

UNDERSTANDING THE PLACE OF THE PROGRAM: WHY THIS NEW PROGRAM AT THIS INSTITUTION AT THIS TIME?

In order to understand your role as a leader of the new academic program process, it is important to investigate the three specific parts of this guiding question:

- **Why this new program?** Perhaps your institution has engaged in some preliminary market research that supports the new program addition or has heard from community partners that a new degree path is warranted. The first question you should address is, why this particular program? That is, why this specific major, academic field, or proposed new program? How is it different from what the institution already offers, and what does it bring that the institution does not already have? Additionally, think about the level and type of credential, degree, or program proposed. Are you offering a new pathway to a new type of degree? Why is it assigned the degree level (i.e., bachelor's, master's, doctoral, micro-credential, graduate certificate, etc.) that it is? How is this level and mode of offering a degree different from what is already offered? And what type of students will the new program attract or seek to educate?
- **At this institution?** Carefully consider the fit of the new program within your institution—what is unique about it (both the institution and the program?), and what is the gap that you are being asked to fill with your leadership and development talent? What struggles or opportunities does your institutional leadership express about the new program development? What language has been used about the need for the program? Is the institution budget-driven or is there some other reason for the new program to emerge? Additionally, consider the type of institution where you work—community colleges offer a different type and style of education than traditional four-year liberal arts colleges because they are designed for different populations and different purposes. Think about why your institution—this particular entity located in your town in your state—is stepping forward with the new program.

- **At this time?** Last, think about the timing of the new program and its development. What sparked the interest from the institution in creating a new academic program? What was going on in the world to prompt administrators or other faculty to recognize a gap in the curriculum and seek to offer a new program? Are there unique student demands? Challenges with the budget? Requests from community employers? Or is a new generational need emerging? The new program does not exist in a vacuum—that is, it was proposed and approved now for a reason—so what is that reason?

Standing alone, each part of this guiding reflective question offers a chance to examine and understand the context of the task to be accomplished. But starting a new academic program at any level requires an answer to each part of the question. That is, without the entirety of why this program at this institution at this time, one would be left on a mission with half of a map. Thus, answering each individual question and then answering the entire question as a whole is necessary in order to understand the purpose of the job in front of you, and without it, new program development might be misguided or misunderstood.

Your Space: Consider this guiding question about starting a new program at your institution. How do you answer each of the following pieces in relation to the work you have been asked to do?

Why this new program? *Think about why your institution is pursuing this particular major or academic program. What seem to be the reasons it has emerged as a priority? What are you hearing/learning/reading about why the institution is willing to expand or change? What is it about this new field or degree offering that is different from what others offer?*

_____

_____

_____

_____

Why at this institution? *What is unique about your institution that makes offering this degree or program something special or unique? What features or attributes does your campus have that make it a good match for this new program? What personnel does your campus house that add expertise to this area? What about the location of your institution—is* *there some reason why this program is best placed at your institution as opposed to elsewhere?*

_____
_____
_____

Why at this time? *What is going on in the academic or professional world that makes this academic or degree program timely? What is it that seems cutting-edge or relevant to today's students? Why now and not five years ago or ten years from now? What is going on in your institution today to warrant adding a new program?*

_____
_____
_____
_____

STANDING IN THE MIDDLE OF CHAOS

The various processes, strategies, and people necessary to start a new program from inception vary from institution to institution, but one thing remains consistent: your presence as a leader of the process. Granted, you might have a team supporting you or some background knowledge to help fill in some gaps, but in the end, the blueprints, design, and architecture of the new program rest on your shoulders.

Yet very few (if any) faculty or academic professionals were brought up in the academy to think in this way—a way that asks them to process innovatively and yet within the boundaries of institutional frameworks. The freedom and exploration that can be present in building a new program can also come with frustration when internal barriers or critics begin to emerge. And, most importantly, most faculty enter higher education with an already-established destination—a major, a desired rank, or a spot to fill—not with the ambition to branch out into program design for a unique major or timely new program. You may suddenly feel out of place.

It is incredibly important, then, that you acknowledge your place in the chaos and excitement that comes with building a new program. You are central to accomplishing this monumental task—from beginning to end. You will imagine the possibilities and acknowledge the challenges. Your role, whether you applied for it or were designated to do it, must be done with purpose and

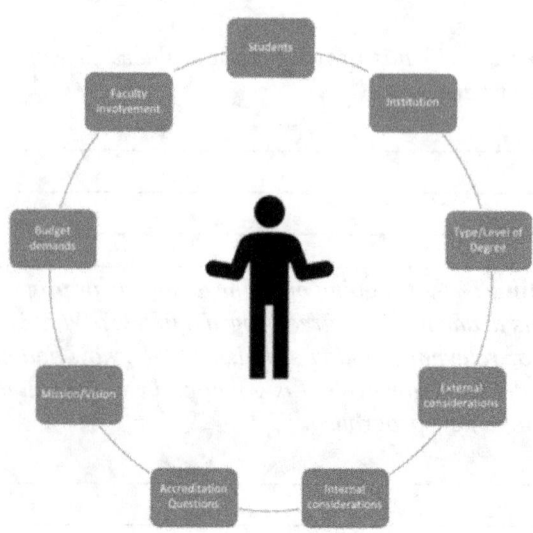

Figure 1.1 Academic Professional as Program Architect Created by Authors

intent. Consider the illustration in figure 1.1, where you, the faculty member, are standing in the center. Study the various constituents, processes, and institutional facets that encompass new program construction.

Each of these different aspects can lead to diverse actions or reactions on the part of the faculty architect/program director. Consider the finer details within each aspect specifically—and note that what we share here are really ideas within each area that barely scratch the surface:

- Students: At the heart of every new program is a desire or need to provide a unique scholarly endeavor for students. The needs of students should, of course, stand at the forefront of every decision made while constructing a program, but these needs may come in different waves at different times. What is it that this new program provides for students? How? And in what way will that be different from other programs already offered?
- Institution: Any institution willing to establish a new program of study, whether it be a degree, major, certificate offering, or even a continuing education course, is certainly the driving force behind the decision-making of the faculty guiding the new program development. The new program must mesh with existing programs, follow suit with institutional requirements, and, overall, benefit the institution as a whole.
- Type/Level of Degree: The type and level of degree challenge the faculty member to hone in on course offerings, objectives, and outcomes—and because many faculty in higher education typically hold graduate degrees (or multiple graduate degrees), this can be a true intellectual exercise in

understanding the leveling of coursework and program outcomes. The faculty architect/program director must understand the distinguishing features of each degree level and how the new program fits within already established institutional structures for how degrees are earned and awarded.
- External Considerations: A new program in and of itself does not exist in a vacuum—thus, a variety of external considerations should be approached. How does the new program fit with the needs of the institutional or even local community? What resources or partnerships could be formed to strengthen the program? And what relationships need to be formed by the program director in order to foster positive partnerships with community members?
- Internal Considerations: Internally, institutional demands like budgeting, marketing, enrollment, admissions, and academic advising all play a role in the successful launch of a program. Faculty building a new program need to intimately understand and work with personnel in a variety of areas outside of their academic silos so as to build the proper functions necessary for a program to roll out.
- Accreditation Questions: Some new programs must consider various accreditation or licensing requirements. Thus, not only is the internal design of the program important, but so too is the alignment with outside requirements set forth by larger organizations. Failure to consider accreditation or licensing requirements while building the program often leads to a program failing to earn accreditation or to the necessity of rebuilding pieces as a means of rectifying deficiencies.
- Mission/Vision: The mission and vision of an institution guides the overall educational direction. Depending on the type of institution you work in, your work might be guided by religious components, mission elements that encourage collaboration or reflective discernment, or even vision statements that provide aspirations for alumni of the institution. Again, building an academic program must consider the mission and vision within the land in which it is being built. Programs that contradict or defy institutional mission or vision are quick to lose support.
- Budget Demands: Money can be a driving force behind why a new program is designed and how it fits the overall structure of an institution. As such, faculty architects/program directors should consider not only the resources necessary to build a program but also to sustain the program. From our experience, we've heard stories of many new program directors who are extremely underfunded not only upon start-up, but throughout the first few years of a new program. You must advocate and account for appropriate resources, whether they be money, faculty, space, or equipment.
- Faculty Involvement: Building a new program may find you as a leader of a new team or working in isolation. Regardless of which end of the spectrum

you fall on, you can learn to network and build relationships with other faculty, both internally and externally, who can help guide the construction process. It is important to realize the stakeholders within the institution—whose areas you might be infringing on, who holds valuable institutional history or knowledge that could assist you in your building processes, or who is available and willing to join you in the program-building process. Additionally, it can be helpful to build a network of faculty outside the institution who have also built a new program in order to utilize their expertise, insights, and even mistakes as a chance to better lead the building process.

In all, when you were identified or appointed to launch a new program, it may have felt like an isolated experience—that you had been given a task too big for one person or one with very little direction or guidance. As you consider your role, standing in the center of the process, also consider the importance of your lived experiences, your role as a student, and your time in the classroom. All of these experiences in academia feed into how you will build a new program and in what ways it will impact an entire generation of students at your institution.

A LEADING AND LEARNING ADVENTURE

If you are like us, it took a while for the magnitude of being tasked with "the launch" to set in. At first, there's the honor of having an idea selected or being the one trusted enough by your leadership to do the job. Then, as ideas begin to spark and excitement starts to build, you also begin to hear the whispers of critics ("Why do we need a new program?" "Why now?" and "Is this really a good idea?"). You start to face the red tape of institutional processes (I need to fill out which form? Why do we do things this way? Who is in charge of what around here?). You begin to realize that resources may be less than promised or that faculty who showed an interest at first have moved on to other projects. The paperwork becomes tedious, yet necessary. Questions lead to more questions, and opportunities lead to new ideas that must be captured for a later date—not now, there's already too much to do. And when those first students step into the classroom, whether it be in-person or virtually, there is the realization that your work is impacting real people, not just imaginary figures in proposal paperwork. With the arrival of students comes new and different challenges from advising, pacing, and coursework alignment. Students need faculty, yet adding faculty can be expensive. Faculty need resources for teaching and research—those, too, come with a price tag. And then there's you—leading all of this from beginning to end.

You are no longer what the world imagines as a professor—the sage on the stage or the researcher buried in experiments and journal articles fades into the past. Instead, you have been transformed into a leader—one who is accountable for the learning of others, for the sustainability of a program, and for integrity as a piece of a larger institution. It's OK—we've been there and survived it. The stories and anecdotes layered within this book reflect both the difficulties and exceptionally rewarding opportunities that come with launching a program. But the first step is to realize that you are stepping out of your comfort zone and into a process that will challenge you, inspire you, and teach you. As you work through these various steps, processes, and undertakings, you will find that you are more versatile and agile than most—and that can be a fantastic discovery to make along the way.

THE CHALLENGE OF SELF-DOUBT

Failure and doubt will also be constant companions as you launch a new program. We speak this from experience as well. Even from those initial moments when you learn you are the one—the one picked, selected, identified—to launch a program, you may also hear your inner critic: Why me? What do I have to offer? What do I know? What if I fail? Let us reassure you that the inner critic, while present, is not always right. But it takes a special kind of person—one willing to see failure as an opportunity, to face the unknown as an adventure, and to work through challenges as puzzles. You have that in you. And we're here to help along the way. Do not let the inner critic cause you to quit, abandon ship, or forget the lives of the students your work will impact. Settle in, work through the process, and know that you are in the right place at the right time—right now.

HOW TO USE THIS BOOK

As we've alluded to throughout this first chapter, this book is a practical guide for faculty and academic practitioners charged with building a new academic program. Our experience lies in building new academic degree programs, majors, certificates, and concentrations at both the undergraduate and graduate levels. We've taken time to talk to some of our colleagues throughout the United States whose work has been different from ours, yet similar in the end goal of building that final academic product. Surprisingly, our experiences have been strikingly similar, which led to the actual need to put these ideas on paper. What you find here is meant to be a guide—not a precise instruction manual, but rather a culmination of how program directors in a variety of programs describe the process of building a program from the ground up. Granted, institutional sizes, missions, types, and structures varied, but some of the main themes emerged: managing the politics surrounding new programs, locating and finding the necessary paperwork to document the building process, learning and understanding unique institutional quirks, and gaining a completely new and unexpected set of skills like creating a budget, hiring staff, or writing an assessment report. In many of our lives, for those of us who have lived and worked in higher education for any period of time, these are the jobs of "others." That is, they have typically not been on our plate—we know they get done, we've witnessed others fret about the processes, but in all, we've never had to invest our own time or energy into understanding what is going on. Program leadership changes this—it shifts the outsider to insider almost instantly. And what was once the comfort of higher education suddenly becomes the unknown.

This book, then, is designed to walk you through the program launch process, from proposal development through assessment planning. It is modeled after processes used at many institutions and encourages you to explore areas with which you may not have anticipated having any involvement. In this process, we will review:

- Proposal development and design
- Managing the politics of institutions
- Building academic processes and structures
- Managing and maintaining reasonable expectations
- Addressing faculty and staff challenges
- Handling ambiguity and adversity
- Advocating for resources
- Assessing and recognizing progress

Each chapter is written as a standalone piece—that is, depending on where you are in the program launch process, you may find jumping from chapter to chapter in a different order or at different times to be the most useful to you. Within each chapter, we share not only our own experiences as program launchers, pieces we've studied about new program development, compiled studying a variety of entities in higher education, conversations captured with others who have launched programs, and evidence-based practices that can help ensure strong program development. We present a variety of real-life examples to help explore challenging questions. Finally, at the end of each chapter, you'll find a list of reflective questions—questions meant for you to consider and explore within the context of where you are today and the institution in which you work. There will be no right answers, but hopefully, these questions will guide you to a deeper, more detailed, and thoughtful approach to your leadership role.

THE PURPOSE OF REFLECTION AND HOW WE WILL GUIDE THIS PROCESS IN THIS BOOK

We would like to take a moment to specifically point out the need for the reflective process and how it impacts a program launch. It is easy to jump into a new responsibility and quickly begin assigning duties, shooting off email requests, and putting words into action. But overall, it is most important to remember the end goal of any program: the student. That is, we must always keep in mind how our decisions today impact our future graduates. In order to do so, we should slow down our processes, as feasible, to explore how and why the design of our program is done in a purposeful manner. This takes time. It means stepping away from the drive to make quick decisions in order to make informed decisions. It also means understanding that what we want as program directors may not be what is best for the students or the institution as a whole. At times during this book, we may prompt you to set aside something you are working on in order to reflect on the how and the why of that work. We hope you will embrace this as an opportunity to pause and consider how your words or actions will impact others.

QUESTIONS FOR YOUR REFLECTION

1. How do you answer the different questions we pose in this chapter: Why this program at this institution at this time?
2. What excites you about this new challenge?
3. What concerns or worries you?
4. Who is someone you can turn to for professional advice during this process?
5. Thinking about your overall workload, where does this new program development fit? What needs to shift in order for you to have enough time in your day to commit to this process?
6. Why you? Think carefully about the skill set you bring to the new program launch process. Which of your talents do you anticipate will be an advantage? Conversely, what gaps or lack of knowledge seem to exist?

Chapter 2

New Academic Proposals

Overview: *This chapter provides a universal framework, descriptions, and a template for new academic program proposals. Based on information, policies, and templates from institutions around the nation, the tools and explanations provided in this chapter will help you, as a faculty program developer and advocate, understand the necessary components for a new academic program proposal and guidance on how to address each area.*

Long before you can begin implementing a new academic program—that is, before building curriculum, hiring faculty, or admitting students—the layout of the new program must be clearly established, defined, and supported with thoughtful processing and information gathering. This includes a detailed market analysis (does the world need this academic program? How will it help our students after graduation? What skills are being taught that cannot be gained elsewhere?) with a convincing rationale (why now? Why here?), data to support the need for the new program on a particular campus or within a particular school (how does our campus support this type of program? How does this new program align with existing majors or degree paths? What sort of tuition income is it expected to generate?), and an overall strategy for finding momentum once the program is approved. Faculty charged with new program design are rarely experts in all of these fields—from marketing to enrollment to budget design to strategic planning. This chapter presents a uniform framework for program proposals based on what we've seen used in colleges and universities across the nation. This tool not only includes commonly required components for new program approval processes, but also some key questions that should be considered when moving from area to area within the proposal. In all, while your institution's new program proposal process may be slightly different or require more or less similar information, using this guide is a good starting point for any faculty member seeking to put together a well-designed plan for further consideration among institutional committees and leaders.

THE NECESSITY FOR PROPER PLANNING

It seems like common sense that any new program proposal would be carefully planned and designed by a knowledgeable expert within the field being proposed. However, reality does not always reflect this practice. At times, campus leaders task a strategic planning committee with uncovering new content areas that could help draw more students to campus. Other times, a faculty member is tapped to design a new program based on their demonstrated experience in curriculum design. Yet in other scenarios, the market pushes an idea into an institution, and a faculty or administrative leader from outside the content area is expected to learn as much as possible about the new area and design a program that lines up with current campus offerings. Regardless of where or how you find yourself in this process, one of the best routines you can engage in, as someone considering or designing a new academic program, is detailed and careful planning. This goes beyond imaginative thinking and instead narrows in on the how and why of the realities of shepherding students from enrollment to graduation. In essence, it is the architecture of the program: the need for the program, the layout of courses, student outcomes, and the overall alignment with institutional goals. In support of good planning, be sure to review your faculty handbook as well as the guidelines for new program proposals and note the timelines and processes required. There will be hard deadlines to follow as well as multiple levels of approvals and reviews as you proceed through the process. Consider speaking with your Dean or Department Chair specifically about the process at your institution and incorporate their feedback and advice. There may be hidden obstacles or campus culture elements that you need to discuss before moving into your proposal.

A UNIVERSAL FRAMEWORK

Using a framework approach allows the program designer to collaborate with others, build a cohesive structure, and collect details along the way in an organized fashion. Some institutions require a specific proposal form or document to be used, but in our work for this book, we've studied, compiled, and synthesized many different approaches into one piece that will meet many of the required components needed to gain institutional support for new program approval. Briefly, these pieces include:

a. Rationale for the new program
b. How the program offers a unique or different perspective to the current academic landscape (need for the program)
c. The potential student market for the proposed program (demand)
d. Program outcomes and alignment with university outcomes
e. Mode of delivery
f. Timeline of implementation
g. List of required courses
h. Assessment procedures
i. Accreditation considerations
j. Existing or projected needed resources

Keep in mind elements will be different at times based on the type of program you are proposing. Graduate programs, for example, may need to include data on undergraduate feeder programs or shared curricula. Proposal types include:

- New Undergraduate Major
- New Undergraduate Minor
- New Master's Degree
- New Doctoral Degree
- New Dual (undergraduate/graduate or graduate/graduate) Degree
- New Credit-Bearing Certificate
- New Non-Credit Bearing Certificate of Achievement

COMPONENTS OF A TYPICAL PROPOSAL

As a program architect, it is important that you have a clear understanding of the various pieces that exist, are needed, or may challenge the implementation of the new program idea. The Universal Framework and its various pieces are intended to help you consider various angles of your idea and to articulate rationales and processes that support new program adoption. In this section, we break down each piece of the Universal Framework to include specific prompts you will want to answer in order to prepare a cohesive and comprehensive program proposal.

Rationale: Preparing a sound rationale is the first step to articulating the vision and potential impact of a new program on a university campus. While it may be daunting, capturing the initial goals, outcomes, and impact of a yet-to-be-adopted program allows others (including potential faculty, students, and administrators) to understand how a new program might complement an institution's landscape of offerings. The rationale should be straightforward and compiled into no more than one page—noting that other details about the proposed program will fall into separate categories of the Universal Framework with more precise details.

The rationale should answer the following prompts, again, in a limited number of words so as not to overwhelm a potential reader and to make a quick and convincing case. A comprehensive rationale will include four parts:

- The title/name/content area of the proposed program
- A description of the learning goals, content, and opportunities
- A clear connection between the proposed program and the existing institutional goals
- The purpose and strengths of the proposed program

Need for the Program: This section explores how creating a new program, at this particular institution, at this particular time, will fill a gap in what students need or want from the institution today. Information in this section might include anecdotal information from alumni, statistics from unfilled jobs in the field, or a documented gap in existing programming. This section should also distinguish how the new program is different from or complements existing programs and/or faculty expertise.

Potential Student Market: New program proposals need to identify the potential to enroll students. We've all considered launching innovative or unique programs that appeal to our own interests, but when we consider building a new program within an institutional structure, there must be some semblance of student demand for the program. Supporting data might come from demand that other institutions have seen with a similar program, information from industry sources regarding potential jobs or job outlook, or even anecdotal demand from existing students. Ideally, the potential student market would be a projection of "if all things go as planned, this is how many students we anticipate enrolling. . ." and over time, growth would occur.

The necessity to gain some understanding of how marketing processes work within higher education is a must for anyone working on a new academic program proposal. Most institutions have a marketing office or some sort of consultant or resource, but few traditional disciplinary faculty interact with these resources in an already-established program. With new academic program development, it is necessary to forge a working relationship with marketing professionals in order to ensure that the new academic program reaches its ideal potential student audience and gains exposure within the academic community.

Abu Noaman with the consulting firm Elliance promoted two specific marketing approaches to help colleges and universities create a positive success ratio for enrollment in new academic programs. The first was making a significant marketing investment so that prospective students can find and learn about the new program (after all, if a potential student can't find the program, how would they ever enroll?). The second was marketing imagination, or pursuing creative or nontraditional marketing strategies (Noaman, 2022).

Faculty leading new academic program proposals and development should be prepared to ask several questions about marketing, including the following:

- What resources does the institution plan to commit to marketing the program? How much of that is "new" money allocated specifically to marketing the new venture?
- What avenues of marketing have worked well for the institution? How can the new program enter these already established pathways?
- What is the overall marketing approach of the institution? Is it to market individual programs based on innovation, potential student interest, or employer job market demands? Or is it to market the institution as a whole and guide potential students to a generalized source of information that then allows a student to explore multiple programs at once?
- Who makes marketing decisions? How much input will you, as the faculty expert, have in assisting with or creating marketing messaging, identifying potential target audiences, or ensuring that messaging reaches the right people?
- How will you know which marketing efforts are successful and which ones struggle? How are marketing results reported and shared within the institution? And how are marketing efforts evaluated for renewal or adjustment?

The Carnegie Higher Education group suggests a strategic approach to marketing new academic programs to ensure web search terms align with program features, that a program has an interesting and inviting landing page, and that multiple sources of audience reach are utilized, including social media channels, organic marketing efforts, and paid digital services (Carnegie, 2018).

Program Outcomes: The academic rigor, challenge, and outcomes for a program should be articulated from early on to ensure that the academic goals of the institution are met with the adoption of each new venture. This includes identifying what students should know or be able to do at the end of the program of study.

Examples:

Mode of Delivery: With the increase of virtual classrooms, course management software, both asynchronous and synchronous learning opportunities, and traditional face-to-face structures, the way a new program is designed to be delivered can range from online to synchronous live classes to learning in a classroom. Each mode of delivery has advantages and disadvantages such as:

- Virtual, online learning:
    - Pros: Accessible to students who may not have access to campus or who live in different areas of the country; less cost-intensive in terms of physical space requirements; can accommodate a variety of scheduling needs; may create more access to subject-matter personnel as instructors;
    - Cons: Requires teaching methods that engage students in online environments; asynchronous learning can sometimes feel disconnected or isolated.
- Traditional, in-person classroom learning:
    - Pros: Students convene with an instructor/faculty to engage in live discussions/applications of content; promotes cohesive learning communities; contributes to the overall campus learning community;
    - Cons: May limit the reach of potential student pool to the local area or those who can take a course only when courses are scheduled; may compete with other content areas of majors.

Student Applications: Getting those first few students in the door of a new academic program takes a bit of awareness and advocacy that, again, most traditionally trained faculty do not readily have. Enrollment management, in and of itself, is a professional field wherein experts study trends in where students go to school, why they select schools, and the landscape of the competition. Many campus enrollment offices are well-oiled machines that specialize in finding students, fine-tuning the messages that convince students to enroll, and ensuring students have a positive experience during their application and enrollment process. As the faculty developer, you may have some input on the application design or process for incoming students—and in that, you should consider how you can make the process easier and functional for all involved. While there are typical components of a student application, there are pieces you may need to decide on when designing how and what students provide in their application. These might include:

- Clear admissions criteria include required GPA, academic skills, credentials, or employment

- Details within the application include background information, work history, and educational institutions attended
- How many and which transcripts are required to gain admission
- The nature of recommendations from others: Do students need professional recommendations or academic ones? Do these recommendations need to be in an original letter or through a form sent out by the institution?
- Documentation of necessary skills, licenses, or other credentials
- A suggested fee for application completion
- A review process, including who will review applications, where, how, and in what timeframe, is essential for effective evaluation.
- A method to determine the quality of candidates
- Structures to communicate with potential students include letters of acceptance or denial
- Processes to begin onboarding once a student is accepted

Student Enrollment: Once a student fits the admission criteria, completes the application, and is accepted into the new academic program, what comes next? Here are some important aspects to think about:

- Will there be a welcome from a faculty member? An orientation session? A series of assignments to complete before the first course?
- How does a student enroll in courses? Where can a student find advice from an advisor? And how is registration handled?
- Who will answer financial aid questions for students? Are there any scholarships or aid available within this particular program?
- Where will students buy their course materials and textbooks? Who will ensure they are properly listed, updated, and available?
- Is there a need for additional background information from the student—perhaps additional prerequisites, an onboarding course, or the need to complete preliminary work?
- What if a student wants to delay enrollment or decides not to attend? How will that be handled?
- Where does communication to students originate? Are there entities within the university, like student affairs, financial aid, the library, or other groups that students need to become familiar with?
- How is retention prioritized after enrollment? How will students stay connected between the time of acceptance into the program until the start of courses?
- How many students can/will you accept into the new program? How will you determine capacity? What happens if demand far exceeds what was originally planned? What happens if demand is much lower than anticipated?
- Are there ways to ensure a diverse admissions pool?

- What automated processes do new students need to be informed about and enrolled in?

It can be impossible to predict all admission and enrollment challenges. Without fail, any new program developer we've worked with has faced an unanticipated challenge with current structures that are hard to update or modify, with enrollment personnel unfamiliar with the nuances of a new program, or with the struggle to get those first few students through the doors. Beyond the academic focus of the program, faculty leading these efforts should make plans to meet with and communicate often with their campus's enrollment and admissions office in order to prevent any missteps or deterrents to admission.

Timeline of Implementation: Timelines can demonstrate implementation goals, key resource phases, or considerations to balance faculty and student needs. One large implementation timeline, from pre-planning stages to assessment of implemented processes, could cover a multiyear period. However, broken into smaller chunks, timelines help the potential audiences engaging with the new program to understand when and how the new program can successfully integrate into institutional processes, when students can access content, and when desired program outcomes can be examined.

Example:
Required Coursework: Within a new program, whether it be a limited credit hour certificate, a new minor course of study, a new undergraduate major, or a graduate degree program, the coursework structure should be decided and aligned with the program's outcomes early on in the proposal process. That is, consider the total amount of credit hours required to complete the program, the number of courses that might fill those credit hour requirements, and any additional activities that students may need to complete in order to earn their program credential. At the time of the proposal, it may be helpful to write a course description (two to three sentences) for each course indicating how the courses fit into the new program and/or what courses need to be developed that do not already exist within the institution's catalog.

Seeing into the Future/Predicting a Program Budget: Identifying, securing, and managing a budget for a new academic program is a complex process that most faculty have little to no training about within their disciplinary expertise. Additionally, costs for a new program can change over time—shifting from start-up costs to continuing costs as a program matures. This is where collaboration with other campus professionals will be necessary. Larry Goldstein, a higher education consultant, identified two areas that new programs need to consider in a financial plan: estimating volume and identifying a comparable example (2016). In his advice about estimating volume,

Goldstein suggested using ranges to posit student enrollment and tuition, taking into account that any program could under- or overestimate student interest and commitment level. Additionally, program costs could vary depending on the start-up costs of securing faculty, curricular materials, or other items necessary to establish a new program. Student enrollment, which is where student tuition is generated, can therefore influence start-up costs. In regard to identifying a comparable example, Goldstein suggests finding a similar program (not necessarily in content, but in size, scope, and function) that might help predict the overall costs of starting and continuing an academic program.

Again, there is no fail-safe accuracy to new program budget design, but there are some key questions that can be asked to begin discussions about revenue, expenses, and overall costs for both start-up and continuing costs. These include

1. How many students can/should the program enroll? What happens to the tuition money once it is collected (are there splits with other campus entities, required contributions to HR costs, additional expenditures necessary?)?
2. What will the costs of hiring and retaining faculty be?
3. Are there any substantial equipment or materials costs to consider?
4. What external costs might be incurred?

A sample budget proposal might include major categories such as costs and expenditures for:

- Faculty (part-time or full-time)
- Graduate assistants
- Support or administrative staff
- Scholarships or awards to be issued
- Technology costs
- Library fees/costs
- Enrollment and marketing expenses
- Supplies and services (including office supplies, necessary subscriptions, and other everyday expenses)
- Physical space acquisition and/or renovation

In all, understanding the entire institutional budget is not necessary to prepare or implement a thoughtful new academic proposal. However, it is more important to have a wide lens on the potential risks and costs of a new program and that each need in a new program does have an associated cost. As a faculty leading this effort, you probably have the best idea of the ideal student-to-faculty ratio, specialized equipment needed for the program, and potential avenues for capturing student enrollment.

Policy Development: New academic programs will automatically fall within the larger university policies and handbooks. The already-established Student Code of Conduct will apply to any new student enrolling. Additionally, institutional policies like Title IX processes, safety protocols, and typical routine functions of the institution will be unaffected by the new program implementation. However, it may be wise to consider a program handbook that lays out specific policies that may be only applicable to students within that new program.

One example we've seen of this is at mostly undergraduate-focused institutions that launch doctoral programs. Doctoral programs, in and of themselves, are simply built differently than undergraduate programs. Doctoral students enroll in higher-level courses, may take fewer courses per semester, and generally have a period where they are enrolled for credit but working independently on a dissertation or final project. These types of programs have benefited from a policy manual or guide that helps students and faculty understand how students in this program might function, fit, or operate differently than what typically happens at the institution. Things to consider in developing a policy manual for a new program might include:

- Continuous enrollment policies
- Grade appeal processes
- Conduct expectations
- Timelines for the completion of degree
- On-campus or online events that are required but not offered for credit
- Outlines or templates of academic products created within the program
- Administrative, advising, and teaching structures

Faculty Hiring: Faculty expertise is the backbone of a strong academic program. Ensuring that faculty are well qualified, prepared to design and develop new curriculum, and able to articulate the importance of growing a new academic program is essential to building a strong foundation. Many new academic programs begin with limited faculty simply because of the unknown potential student enrollment and tuition revenue. However, understanding the costs and benefits of hiring faculty is a basic premise that all program developers should understand.

The cost of hiring or retaining a faculty member can vary based on several factors: disciplinary expertise, competition with hiring professionals from nonacademic jobs, recruitment costs, relocation costs, and expenses for typical employee benefits (retirement contributions, health insurance, etc.). Retaining faculty can include expenses like increasing salary, office supplies, travel, and research support.

Things for faculty developing new academic programs to consider might include

- How many faculty are necessary to start the program? What conditions need to be present to justify hiring additional faculty in the future?
- Does the disciplinary expertise of faculty needed for the program cost more than other programs due to the specialized training of the faculty, market demand, or availability of qualified educators?
- What are the expectations from the institution on utilizing already-present faculty or staff? Will existing jobs shift to provide support for the new academic program? Will compensation structures need to change or budget lines need to move?
- Is promotion and tenure inherent in faculty positions within the new program? If so, what support is present for these processes? If not, how will that change faculty recruitment efforts?

Identifying and finding faculty can be a challenge, both in finding faculty willing to work at the beginning stages of an untested program and in retaining faculty during periods of unpredictable enrollment. Some professionals are ripe for the challenge, while others prefer the stability of more traditional faculty roles. As a new academic program developer, your role is to be cognizant of the need for the right disciplinary expertise in faculty, a good fit for the program, and finding someone you can work alongside as growing pains and change occur.

Other Resources: The types of resources needed to build a new program are varied, so you will want to consider not only potential financial needs, but also the demands on faculty time, existing program resources, materials needed, space or institutional resources required, or additional pay requirements. At the outset, this may seem like guesswork, but it is better to estimate the potential for expenses than to face a situation where you face expenses but no allocated resources.

Assessment Processes: When working on a new academic program proposal, it can be difficult to look into the future to fully consider the assessment processes that will need to be in place once faculty are in position, students arrive, and courses are offered. However, assessment is one of the most important components in ensuring a program is strong, fruitful, and doing what it was designed to do. Assessment in higher education can take place at multiple levels, from university-wide assessment to college-level assessment to department-level assessment to program assessment. Assessment is essentially examining your program outcomes to determine if students know or accomplish learning what they were supposed to during their time in the program. This typically requires analyzing student grades on specific assignments that can adequately measure an outcome and determining where there might be gaps in achievement or content offered.

Accreditation Considerations: Some new academic programs will need to be aligned with local, state, or national accreditation standards. These overarching entities generally focus on evaluating the educational standards and processes within an academic discipline. For example, the American Association of Colleges and Schools of Business (AACSB) is an international accrediting institution for many business colleges and programs throughout the world. The organization provides quality assurance, learning resources, and accreditation options. While accreditation is sometimes a voluntary process, it can be a sign of prestige and an affirmation that the program or institution has met industry standards or professional benchmarks. Additionally, in some disciplines, accreditation is required to qualify for or receive government funds. When an institution receives AACSB accreditation, it is a testament that the institution "demonstrates an ongoing commitment to excellence in teaching, research, curriculum development, and learner success" (AACSB, 2024).

Some new academic programs will not fall under required or suggested accreditation processes. As the faculty member leading the development and implementation of a new academic program, it will be extremely important to understand if there are any required accreditation processes needed, the organizations that oversee the accreditation process, and what pieces the new program will need to have in place to earn accreditation. Elements of this might include a specific student-to-faculty ratio, a set of required courses or content to be taught, or even the allocation of proper resources to support the program. Depending on the organization overseeing accreditation, program personnel should be prepared to submit documents detailing course descriptions, student plans of study, assessment processes, and even components of a self-study from the first few years working with students.

COMPREHENSIVE PROPOSAL ELEMENTS

The following pages detail aspects of a new academic proposal with a vast array of resources. These areas were derived from a comprehensive review of proposal requirements from a variety of institutions and colleges of varying sizes and academic focuses. It is unlikely you will be required to include all of these elements, and you should follow the guidelines provided by your institution. However, you may use this comprehensive collection as a guide when considering your approach and the information you will need to compile and review for your proposal. We've left some space on each page for you to take notes, draft outlines, or think about specific components of planning that will help ensure you've worked through a meaningful planning process. Your proposal guidelines will likely be found on your Provost or Chief Academic Officer's web page.

SECTION 1: PROGRAM DESCRIPTION

Craft one paragraph that provides a broad overview of the program. Include general information about program content, faculty roles, and career possibilities for students. Include information about how the program will benefit the institution as a whole.

Additionally, describe how the program might draw prospective students, meet the needs of potential employers, or align with the overall university's vision or mission.

SECTION 2: RATIONALE FOR THE PROGRAM (NEED AND JUSTIFICATION)

> Why this program?
>
> How does this program build on institutional strengths, and how is it consistent with the overall aims of the institution?
>
> How does the new academic program connect to or strengthen the institution's mission, vision, and/or strategic plan?

SECTION 3: EVIDENCE OF NEED FOR THE PROGRAM

- What local or regional labor needs does the program help fill?
- Are there local experts that can help guide the content development so as to meet a particular expertise in the job market?
- What local, national, or regional studies provide evidence of need in this area?
- What key supporters will provide insights into the program's needs? Are there alumni or friends of the program that might advocate for it on your behalf at board or budget meetings?
- Identify trends in the job market, employee needs, and/or potential community growth that might benefit from this program.

SECTION 4: POTENTIAL COSTS OF A NEW PROGRAM

Faculty and Staff

> Consider the number of faculty and staff that will be needed to build a strong program. This might include part-time, adjunct, limited-term, or student workers that can help align processes, build courses, and/or meet with constituents during the growth phase.

Facilities

> Investigate what facilities will be required for the new program. Will it need physical space? Lab space? A new building? A redesign of old or unused space? Estimate costs not only for the physical occupation of space but also for the equipment and supplies needed to make the area functional for work.

Other Capital Costs (e.g., Equipment)

> Capital costs might include lab equipment, printing supplies, specialized equipment, technology upgrades, or innovative classroom teaching materials.

Support
Nature of Support (New, Existing, or Reallocated)

> Conduct a survey to better understand where existing resources might be reallocated to support the new program, where costs might be overestimated, or where other programs have experienced budget challenges as growth occurred

Anticipated Support Channels
Take into consideration any potential donor money, research influx, or community contributions.
Proportion of salary of any faculty member who would contribute to the program (figure 2.1).

Sample Budget Template:

Personnel	
Faculty (Include FTE)	
Graduate Assistants (Include FTE)	
Support Staff (Include FTE)	
Fellowships/Scholarships	
Operating Expenses	
Materials	
Other Resources	
Materials	
Professional fees	
Supplies and Services	
Equipment	
Other Expenses	
Physical Facilities	
Office space/facilities	
Renovations	
Other Expenses	
	GRAND TOTAL

Figure 2.1 Sample Budget Template. *Source*: Created by Authors.

SECTION 5: SIMILAR AND RELATED PROGRAMS

Similar Programs

What programs already exist that might be similar to or aligned with the new program you are developing? It's possible there may be emerging programs within your own institution or nearby. Capture the landscape of trends at your own institution and those that draw students similar to the ones your program will draw.

SECTION 6: PREPARATION FOR ONGOING EDUCATION

Identify how students that engage in the new program might also be prepared to enter other disciplinary areas or programs of study. Specifically:

- Are students that need to pursue further education (like a graduate degree) prepared to apply to and succeed in a graduate program?
- Will credits within the program transfer to other programs, or can the credits be used toward multiple degree requirements?
- Are there possibly collaborative or articulation agreements that might strengthen the enrollment potential of the new program? How can those opportunities be solidified?

SECTION 7: QUALITY AND OTHER ASPECTS OF THE PROGRAM

Quality

Identify how the new program will meet not only program and institutional requirements but in a meaningful way. How will quality be determined? Who will oversee and check on the quality of the coursework and processes of the program? And what checks and balances can be put in place from the beginning to provide quality assurances?

Indicate courses to be included in the program.

Compile a list of courses that will lay out the foundation of a student's plan of study. Identify any courses that may be duplicative of other courses in the institution or that may be used across disciplines.

Design a student's plan of study, or progression through the program, including which courses need to be taken in sequence, which courses can be taken at any time in the program, and/or any experiential or internship courses the student may need to complete.

Clearly identify credit hour allotments, how those credit hours will be monitored, and the assessment techniques that will be used to understand what students are learning throughout their coursework.

Program Learning Outcomes

Craft learning outcomes for the program. Align those with the institutional outcomes and ensure that the program outcomes directly support the institutional outcomes in practice. Also, ensure that any accreditation or licensing outcomes are articulated if necessary.

Assessment

Summarize how the program will assess student knowledge through coursework, learning experiences, student feedback, or other processes.

Placement of Graduates

Describe the potential jobs or occupational paths graduates from the program may be able to pursue after graduation. If students will need postgraduate training, where and how might that occur, and how will this program/institution support the student's application? Finally, specify career development resources that will be available to students in this program—from resume development to building a connection with a professional mentor.

Perceived Institutional Challenges

Articulate any perceived or real challenges that are present as you've developed this proposal. Where have questions arisen already? What areas are you noticing might need institutional direction in order to partner with this program? What customs or traditions might make it difficult to adopt a new program?

SECTION 8: ANTICIPATED STUDENT ENROLLMENT

While it can be difficult to anticipate exactly how many students will apply for and be admitted to any new degree program, think more broadly about how you will find students, what qualifications they will need to gain admission, and any special considerations the institution might have, including the need to move or to find full-time employment during a program. Identify how many full-time and part-time students would make the program feasible and reasonable. Enrolling too many students can cause courses to be too full or faculty to face difficulties in teaching, yet enrolling very few students might create courses with limited engagement or promise for sustainability.

QUESTIONS FOR YOUR REFLECTION

1. Looking at the various pieces of a new program proposal, what do you find most challenging? Why? Where can you find support to help build that piece?
2. Thinking about your own institution, how can you best understand the things you don't know (budgets, finance, allocation of resources)?
3. What opportunities does starting a new program provide for your university?
4. Consider what it will be like for a student enrolling in your new academic program. What advantages or disadvantages might be readily apparent? How can you create a meaningful student experience?
5. Many facets of the Universal Program Proposal require input from others with whom you may have never worked before during your academic time. What background knowledge would be helpful to build as you forge these relationships? Where might you gain information to better help these relationships be fruitful?

Chapter 3

Political Maneuverings and Persuasive Language (Internal and External Stakeholders, Collaboration, and Political Considerations)

Overview: One aspect of new academic program design is the complexity and number of internal and external stakeholders involved in the process. Thoughtful planning and market research are essential to understanding the local/regional landscape and the campus-based and community relationships that must be cultivated in order to create a robust new academic program. Part of building relationships is dependent on political talent and the ability to gain support. This chapter explores internal and external stakeholders, key campus constituents, developing political skills, as well as ideas to engage community stakeholders in the new program design.

New program design can be an exciting time of intellectual and academic expansion—one in which new ideas are welcomed, the ability to design learning seems organic, and the creation of a new project can fill one's bucket for creative scholarly activity. As refreshing as this process can be, it can also be fraught with political challenges from outsiders (and insiders) who challenge new program development, its role in innovation on a campus, and the need for new programming among other programs that might be struggling for infrastructure investment.

Often, the impetus for new program design and development is based on one of the following: (a) demands in the job market for a certain type or skill that graduates can fill; (b) competition with other colleges or universities that are able to recruit new students with new programming; (c) emerging opportunities for improved funding, both internal and external, that support program growth; and/or (d) faculty expertise that can capture students in new and unique ways. Thus, new programs are generally ones that have some sort of economic incentive for development, offer the promise of engaging or enrolling additional students in the institution, or provide an angle for the college or university to create something unique in the current market of majors and minors.

Money, then, cannot be ignored as a key piece of new program development. Colleges and universities are reluctant to develop new programs that will not, in turn, produce a financial benefit to the overall institution. Additional tuition revenue, possible grant funding influx, and a drive for alumni and community financial support can help secure that a new program will be a benefit and not a burden to the institution. However, beyond finances, other political challenges arise that new program developers should carefully consider as development is taking place. These include the nature of the "academic capitalist regime," how "the market" drives academic decisions, politics on campus, the voices of stakeholders, natural resistance to change, and the need for collaboration rather than siloed efforts.

UNDERSTANDING THE "ACADEMIC CAPITALIST REGIME"

While higher education institutions are typically thought of as somewhat untethered by the demands and pressures of the corporate world, in many ways they have taken on corporate structures to survive in today's competitive environment. Kevin McClure, associate professor of higher education at the University of North Carolina at Wilmington, defined academic capitalism as a way for colleges and universities to adjust to external pressures facing institutions today, from reduced government funding to the growing global economy (Koenig, 2019). McClure noted that the academic capitalist theory suggests that colleges and universities have "responded through market and market-like activities, trying to figure out new ways to bring in revenue to make up for some of those cuts in state funding" (para. 8).

Today's institutions are having to consider more than what students want; they must also include budgetary challenges, market drive for graduates, and the potential for programs to generate revenue. Additionally, there is evidence to suggest that successful programs "better align student interest with success in the job market after graduation" (Adame, 2023, para. 9). Implementing new academic programs is risky—institutions face losing not only initial development investments but also buy-in from campus critics, a lack of strong alignment with the job market, and a dearth of faculty who are trained to innovate and create rather than research and teach.

THE MARKET-DRIVEN CULTURE OF ACADEMIA

The market for higher education rests in the hands of two main constituencies: students who want or need education and employers who seek students with education or expertise in a given area. The global higher education market size was estimated at $736.80 billion in 2023 (Grand View Research, 2024). Typically, colleges' and universities' main sources of income are student tuition and fees. In addition to this, research grants, contracts, and opportunities for corporate partnerships also bring significant money into an institution. Balance this, though, with the costs of paying faculty and administrator salaries, maintaining a campus, marketing and advertising, and overall business operations, and the margins for profit can be relatively slim. Thus, venturing into new program development, with an average investment cost of $500K–$2M within the first four years, and it makes sense that institutions may tread into these new ventures with caution.

However, new programs can also breathe life into a struggling or dying institution. A report by Lightcast noted that new programs need not be the most cutting-edge to succeed. The study stated, "Humanities programs in general do not fail significantly more than STEM programs, meaning that the door to success is open to everyone" (Adame, para. 4). This is a promising highlight for faculty building new programs in that new programs need to be more aligned with the university's goals, mission, and graduate outcomes more so than meeting an immediate need for graduates with a particular skill within a narrow industry.

Competing for students can also be a costly venture. In 2021, the *Washington Post* reported that a SimpsonScarborough survey found that institutions spend between $429 and $623 per enrolled student, per year, on marketing alone (Marcus, 2021). Colleges collectively spent around $2 billion on advertising in 2018, including things like sponsorships, promotional ventures, and advertising (Marcus, 2021). It is not tenable for an institution to not participate in an aggressive marketing effort. In order to compete in the market—that of universities and colleges competing for students—an institution must have a plan to not only reach potential students but also to also retain students once they enroll in a program.

New academic programs are not a guaranteed route to income or prestige for an institution. Thus, while we argue for expedited processes to facilitate new program adoption and implementation, care must also be exercised to protect the integrity of the program, the reputation of faculty champions, and the need to exercise financial responsibility. A new program is more than putting a good idea into action; it also involves creating a structure for sustaining said program, engaging students in meaningful and productive ways, supporting faculty growth and development, and aligning any new program with existing university goals, mission, and vision.

MISSION, VISION, AND STRATEGIC PLANNING: BUILDING ON EXISTING FOUNDATIONS

Three processes common to most institutions of higher education are mission, vision, and strategic planning. As a faculty member, you have probably taken part in mission-based activities, providing information on how your discipline can inform the vision of the institution's future, and may have even taken part in the strategic planning process. These pieces are unique to each institution—no two look alike, and regarding new program development, each element should be carefully considered when thinking about program design, student outcomes, and the overall role of the program within the institution. Leadership scholar Peter Drucker once stated, "That business purpose and business mission are so rarely given adequate thought is

perhaps the most important cause of business frustration and failure" (Drucker, 2009, p. 31). Because each of these areas is unique in and of itself, thinking about how a new program may impact the growth or reputation of an institution, how the vision and mission are aligned with the new program, or where the program might help an institution fulfill its mission is an integral piece of planning. Here are some key points to reflect on when assessing a new program's fit within these three structures:

Vision: The vision of an institution "represents future purpose, providing a mental picture of the aspirational existence that an organization is working toward" (Horwath, para 2). That is, the vision is a look into the future—where the institution hopes to be in the coming years and the impact it seeks to make within education many years down the road. You'll often see words like "aspires to," "seeks to," and "promotes"—all written in future tense. Here are two examples of vision statements found on University websites:

- Harvard College looks into the future with its vision statement by sharing, "Harvard College sets the standard for residential liberal arts and sciences education. We have committed to creating and sustaining the conditions that enable all Harvard College students to experience an unparalleled educational journey that is intellectually, socially, and personally transformative" (Harvard College, 2024, para. 2).
- Auburn University: "To lead and shape the future of higher education" (Auburn University, 2024, para. 1).

Building and offering a new academic program should align with an institution's vision from the outset. If the program does not fit what the organization is hoping to be in the future, there is a clear conflict of interest. Consider, for example, if a new program were adopted at Harvard College that did not promote personal transformation. This would clearly not be a step forward for the institution and would be difficult to promote as something that would strengthen the future of the organization if it were working in contrast to its stated vision.

Mission: A mission is a "clear, concise and enduring statement of the reasons for an organization's existence today" (Horwath, para 2). Contrasting the mission with the vision of an organization, where the vision is aspirational and based in the future, the mission statement is what we, as an institution, are doing today to fulfill our purpose. Mission statements are written with active verbs ("to be" "is dedicated") rather than future-tense verbs. Additionally, a mission statement is something that can be studied today, thought about in terms of what actions, processes, or steps we are actively taking to move towards the vision. Here are two examples of mission statements from higher education institutions:

- Harvard Business School: "to educate leaders who make a difference in the world" (Harvard Business School, n.d., para. 1).
- North Carolina State University's mission reads, in part, that the university "is dedicated to excellent teaching, the creation and application of knowledge, and engagement with public and private partners" (North Carolina State University, 2024, para. 1).

A new academic program must consider the institution's mission. If a new academic program at Harvard Business School were to espouse "to educate leaders whose personal fulfillment is the primary focus of their work," the institutional mission would be in jeopardy.

Strategic Plan: Nearly every institution of higher education has a strategic plan in place, and as a faculty member, you may have played a role in helping formulate, design, or implement a strategic plan. Catherine Cote, a marketing coordinator at Harvard Business School Online, defined a strategic plan as "ongoing organizational process of using available knowledge to document a business's intended direction" (2020, para. 1). In this plan, an organization sets specific goals, creates measurable outcomes, and implements an assessment process that determines if the goals were met during a set period. In this planning, considerations for personnel allocation, resources, time, and other institutional priorities emerge. Strategic plans generally have a life cycle in which design, implementation, and assessment take place over several years. When that cycle is complete, most institutions engage in another strategic planning process for another set interval of years. A new academic program, whenever proposed and implemented, will likely fall into a strategic planning cycle—and perhaps might help the institution meet the goals of the strategic plan.

WHAT DOES THIS ALL MEAN WHEN DEVELOPING A NEW ACADEMIC PROGRAM?

Proposing, designing, and implementing a new academic program means that the work you do does not exist in isolation. It automatically becomes part of the larger institution—no matter how functional or disheveled that institution may be. The organization's mission, vision, and strategic plans are all structures you must work alongside and in concert with in order not only fit within the institution but to create the potential for long-term success.

As the new academic program advocate, you can strengthen your work by clearly accounting for, articulating, and explaining how the new program fits within these three key areas of the institution. How will the new program help serve the mission today? In what ways can the new program help achieve the aspired goals of the vision? And strategically, how does the new program fit within the things the institution is building, improving, or strengthening today? Prepare your proposal and any associated documentation to share with stakeholders to outline specifically how the new program is a good fit and already, even before welcoming the first student, is a natural fit to be offered at your institution.

BARRIERS TO NEW PROGRAM DEVELOPMENT: INTERNAL VS. EXTERNAL

New program development can sometimes be wrought with barriers from people, processes, and structures within the institution. Tracy Schoolkraft from Shippensberg University compiled a list of five common barriers to new program development in her article titled "Overcoming Barriers to New Program Development" (2016). These include: (a) the red-tape within an institution that slows down adoption and approval (paperwork, budget needs, etc.); (b) the lack of faculty expertise in new program design, business issues, or marketing needs; (c) an inherent unwillingness to find willing faculty to launch new programming because it does not fit neatly within typical research, teaching, and service roles necessary for rank and promotion; (d) the need for new programs to cross interdisciplinary lines;

and (e) the need to shift to an entrepreneurial mindset rather than a stalwart academic one.

What Dr. Schoolkraft identified in her work was that within new program development, often, the most immediate hurdles are from within the institution. Institutional leaders can help alleviate some of these barriers by providing expedited review processes, supporting faculty innovation through specific campus support within the rank and promotion process, and building structures that foster collaborative work between and among departments, programs, and academic fields.

In addition to internal barriers, external barriers may also stall the development of a new program. This might include competing institutions offering similar or identical programming more quickly, community partners being unwilling to support new program development, or even potential job sources for graduates suddenly drying up or dying. Occasionally, an institution will face a challenge from its own ranks—faculty who do not see a need for a new program, alumni who challenge the viability of such programming, or enrollment departments that are unable to articulate how to locate and sell new programming to students.

THE LAYERS

One facet commonly encountered by new academic program leaders is the layers that exist within institutions of higher education. Depending on population, overall institutional size, definitions of faculty roles, and political influences, most colleges and universities host a similar alignment of power structures.

New ideas are generated at all layers within an institution, but generally cannot be carried out without the approval of the other layers. For instance, if a faculty member proposes offering a new course within the English department, generally, not only will the English department need to approve the new course, but so too will the college, and ultimately the university/college. It is best to consult your faculty handbook and academic program review committee guidelines for the specific steps and approval levels at your institution to ensure that you are aligned with the processes and procedures your institution might require (figure 3.1).

Within each of these larger bodies, there are also structures and processes within individual offices or programs that may create additional layers of approvals for a new program. These offices might be those of Associate Deans, Curriculum Committees, Academic Policy Committees, or Financial Oversight Committees.

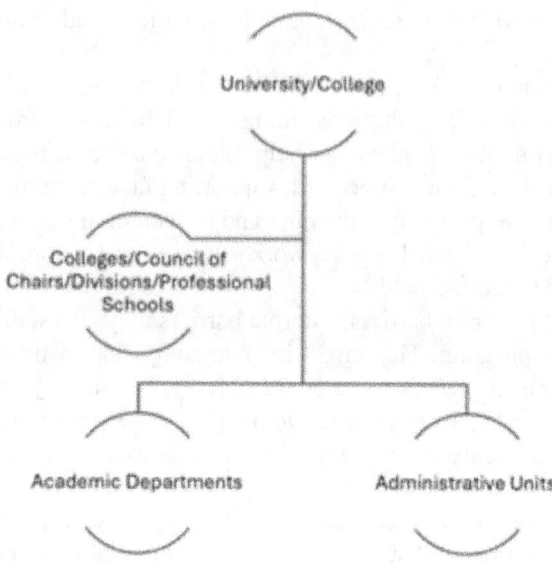

Figure 3.1 Typical Layers of a College or University's Approval Processes

Additional Groups/Offices/People Who May Require Independent Review of a New Program:

- Dean's Council
- President or Provost's Council
- Faculty Senate or Governing Body
- Marketing Department
- Enrollment Management Department
- Instructional Design Department
- Legal Office/General Counsel
- Libraries
- Human Resources
- Curriculum Committee
- Budget Committee
- School or College
- Department
- Department Chair or College Dean

THE ROLE OF STAKEHOLDERS

The stakeholders involved in new program development are both internal and external. Consider how these lists compare (figure 3.2):

The various needs, demands, and desires of stakeholders do not fit neatly within this box, however. For example, the demands of the student body to gain a major in a new technology may not mirror the skills that an employer is seeking in new graduates. Alternatively, the demands of a community group to create mission-aligned programming may undermine the availability of faculty or staff to lead such a program. How, then, does a new program developer consider the needs of stakeholders in the development process?

We propose a series of **five questions** that every new program developer should ask specifically about stakeholders in relation to the program being built:

(a) **What drives the stakeholders' interest in the new program?**

It may be that a stakeholder is resistant to change simply because it shifts attention from an existing program to a new area—thus, causing worry that new programs will overtake established areas of the institution. It could be that a stakeholder sees a financial benefit from investing in a new program

Figure 3.2   Stakeholders in the New Academic Proposal Process

early, hoping for a potential grant partnership or employment benefit. Examining stakeholder interests is not always easy but is essential to understanding whose voice should be listened to and whose voice can be shifted to the background.

(b) **Are the stakeholder's interests clearly aligned with the new program's goals and outcomes?**

If a stakeholder's interest is not aligned with the educational goals or outcomes of a new program, conflicts will eventually arise. A misalignment may be in the design of a new program (face-to-face vs. virtual), in the intended target student population (for example, traditional undergraduate students versus professionally employed graduate students), or in the content offered in the new program (for example, technical skills versus more theoretical understandings of an industry). Additionally, a mission-type conflict may occur when a stakeholder seeks to engage in processes or practices that are not educationally sound or that are contrary to the institution's moral or ethical position.

(c) **How can working closely with the stakeholder help or harm the new program?**

New programs tend to attract a buzz around campus because they signify change. This may attract the attention of supporters or detractors. Stakeholders have the potential to be helpful to the program by offering skilled assistance, professional guidance, financial means, or political support. In contrast, stakeholders may also serve as detractors to innovation, individuals with micromanaging tendencies, or potential pseudo-hostage situations, withholding support unless a certain set of wants or desires is fulfilled. Weigh the need for support carefully—and consider whether the support of a particular group or individual will help the program development through meaningful engagement or hurt program development through needless distractions.

(d) **What specifically is the stakeholder seeking to gain from the new program?**

Working alongside a stakeholder, whether internal or external, can be a strong source of encouragement for faculty developing new programs. However, it is important to understand the motivations of any stakeholder. Are staff members volunteering time in the hopes of finding a new role or position (unpromised) within the new program? Are alumni engaged because the potential graduate funnel will improve the economic outlook of their own company?

It seems demeaning to say that all stakeholders will have something to gain from new program development, but it is essential that the question be asked in order to ascertain conflicts of interest, potential challenges to program development, and interpersonal situations that could become uncomfortable should the relationships not be as fruitful as hoped.

(e) **How can a long-term relationship with the stakeholders benefit students and faculty in the new program?**

Partnering with stakeholders, both internal and external, can also be a tremendous benefit to the faculty developer and future students and faculty of a new program. Stakeholders may offer support through personal skills, time in development, intellectual expertise in an area that faculty may not be strong in, or in creating opportunities for students to connect with the new program. Long-term relationships with stakeholders can help build a pipeline for employment, provide stability in creating processes for enrollment and retaining students, and may solidify the academic rigor of a new venture.

RESISTANCE TO CHANGE

Change is an inevitable part of new program development on any campus. Change is encompassed in the processes that investigate new majors or academic pursuits, redefine faculty roles, and challenge the siloed nature of higher education. Scholar India Lane identified a series of factors that contribute to resistance to change in higher education. These include a lack of perceived need for change; strong traditions; conservative educational practices, autonomy of individuals; disciplinary identification by faculty; and fear of the unknown (2007).

Change, it seems, causes a pause for most individuals in that it means things are not remaining as expected or desired. While change can sometimes be exciting and inspiring, it can also be challenging and exhausting. Lane went on to suggest solutions to help overcome change in higher education—and we've identified several of those as particularly relevant to new program development. These include conveying the need for the change; assessing levels of resistance; appealing to both intellectual and emotional concerns; encouraging wide participation; ensuring sufficient time for change to be implemented; and, most importantly, creating a strong proposal. That is, one of the best ways to overcome resistance to change is to have a strong plan from the outset. This lies in the hands of the faculty developer (2007).

Specifically in relation to new program development, change can occur in expected and unexpected ways, from the voices of unexpected critics to the applause of alumni who see the university changing to meet the needs of a current demand. How can a faculty developer best handle the change at their feet? Here are our suggestions:

a. **Embrace change**: Be aware that it sometimes causes a natural human resistance that may or may not be vocalized. You need to be secure in the changes that will occur when a program you develop is approved. When developing a program proposal, indicate where change is needed and why, but also point out the existing structures that need to stay in place for a program to succeed. Point out the strengths of what the institution is already doing—not just the need for upheaval.
b. **Communicate with clarity:** As a program developer, articulating the need for a new program may begin to feel extremely repetitive as you encounter a new audience or someone unfamiliar with what is taking place. Be prepared with a two- to three-sentence overview of what the new program is, why it is needed at this institution, and how you see students benefiting from the program. For example, our colleague championing a new cybersecurity program at a small college once had his "elevator speech" down to a few simple statements to the effect of "Our college preparing students in cybersecurity is not only meeting the needs of the employers we work closely alongside, but is also providing space for the critical thinking, ethical debates, and preparation for issues that can arise in any industry in the next two decades."
c. **Communicate frequently:** As a program developer, it is easy to become isolated in the development process. After all, you are the one thinking about curriculum options and program outcomes. However, you can gain support and buy-in by communicating frequently with stakeholder groups. Share program outcomes as they are written. Promote new coursework and identify how it will bring new energy to the campus. Invite ideas from faculty and staff working in already functional programs.
d. **Recognize your weaknesses and seek advice:** As a new program developer, recognize that you do not have all the answers. Be transparent about this with your stakeholders. When you do not know how to do something or how a particular institutional process occurs, ask someone who does. Build trust by seeking sound input from others. Not only will you strengthen the program you are designing, but you will gain personal support from others working throughout the institution who may already be doing what you seek to do in an established program.

THE HIGH COST OF INNOVATION

New academic program development was called a "bad bet" in a 2024 report from the market research firm Burning Glass. Their report, "Bad Bets: The High Cost of Failing Programs in Higher Education," analyzed graduation data for the 10,536 new undergraduate and graduate degree programs that were launched in 2010–2011 Light. In 2018, the firm looked at which programs had done well and which had succumbed to failure. Fifty percent of programs launched during the academic year 2010–2011 had failed by 2018 in that they were graduating less than five students. Thirty-three percent of the programs were considered successful in that they were graduating more than ten graduates per year. There was no clear pattern as to what made a program succeed or fail—majors from all fields had both some potential for risk and success. However, the firm noted one startling number: the average cost of sustaining a new program over four years was roughly $2 million (Burning Glass, 2020).

An institution is wise to adopt new programs with careful consideration due to the financial burden alone, but that must also be balanced with the need for expedited launch processes (to meet immediate needs in the market demand), the support of faculty, who, after all, are highly skilled in their academic fields, and the challenge of enrolling new students into a program with no clear history to it.

ORGANIZATIONAL CULTURE

Organizational culture can be defined in multiple ways but generally includes values, behaviors, attitudes, systems, beliefs, and rules that influence employee behavior and create the overall working conditions or perceptions about the institution. Institutions of higher education actually maintain multiple cultures on and off campus that encompass students, staff, faculty, administration, alumni, and athletics. In terms of our work on program development, we must consider the impact of both written and unwritten aspects of institutional culture. Politics is always present, and awareness of institutional politics will help facilitate a process free of unintended consequences or complications.

How might institutional culture impact your process? One way is through budgeting and resource allocation. Most institutions are analyzing budgets and resources carefully and are looking for efficiencies and unnecessary duplication of efforts or redundancies. You may encounter colleagues who have not been successful in attempts to propose new programs or who have had budget cuts in their department. They may view your work in a negative light, even if it has nothing to do with the quality of your proposal. When resources are limited, people tend to guard what they have, and the culture becomes one where community members are less collaborative or even hostile to other areas.

Another area of culture could be described as power and control. Higher education is very hierarchical, and issues of power are always at play. Should your proposal require collaboration and support from other departments, programs, or faculty, you must carefully employ your best teamwork skills to build buy-in from these constituents. We've seen solid proposals face rejection due to personality conflicts of faculty or quite simply a lack of collegiality and manners. Consider inviting people you need into your design process so they may offer ideas and feedback. Assuming it's an honest process, this will help diffuse power dynamics and build a coalition. It never hurts to model good practice with the assumption that you wish to build a culture of respect and collegiality.

Finally, you must think about everyone who will be affected by your proposal or who will be a part of the review process. Are there any relational dynamics that could get in the way? When you work with people, past issues are always present, so try to prepare for any complications that could arise from relationships between individuals, departments, or colleges. If your proposal requires input or support from outside constituents, be sure to do your homework and vet any prior or existing relationships they may have with other departments or entities on campus.

COLLABORATION AS AN ESSENTIAL DEVELOPMENT SKILL

In summary, new program development is not always about exciting new courses or a guaranteed job funnel for graduates. New programs can and will fail, so you need to work with that reality in place. Additionally, a new program, while it may seem like only an intellectual investment by an institution, can also be a challenging financial investment. Add to these challenges the unique needs and demands of stakeholders, both internal and external, and being a new program developer seems more like winning a political battle than building an academic process.

A willingness to collect and share ideas, to listen to the needs and desires of stakeholders, and to learn from others is a critical skill for any new program developer. While you may have ideas on why a program is needed or how it will be successful, it is equally important to build buy-in from those on campus and those with campus interests. This means stepping back, considering the larger picture of how an institution runs in today's world, and how the individuals that help that institution run each day fulfill the daily roles of processes and purpose.

QUESTIONS FOR YOUR REFLECTION

1. What is your personal reaction to change? How can you navigate your potential personal resistance to change in order to champion a new program?
2. Who are your internal stakeholders? What skills, knowledge, or attributes do they bring to help you build a new program?
3. Who are your external stakeholders? How can you best assess their interests and willingness to support your efforts?
4. How can you help overcome the skepticism or discomfort that happens with change at your institution? What can you do to promote stability and belief in the program you are developing?
5. What risks and opportunities is your institution embracing by allowing new program development to take place? How can you acknowledge these risks in a meaningful way? How can you mitigate the risks?

SUGGESTED READINGS

Diallo, L. & Gerhardt, K. (2017). Designing academic leadership programs: Emerging models. *Journal of Leadership Education, 16*(2), 92–108.

Dee, J. R. & Heineman, W. A. (2016). Understanding the organizational context of academic program development. *New Directions for Institutional Research, 2015*(168), 9–35.

Kezar, A. (2018). *How colleges change: Understanding, leading, and enacting change.* Routledge.

Kezar, A. & Lester, J. (2009). *Organizing higher education for collaboration: A guide for campus leaders.* Jossey-Bass.

Milkovich, A. (2016, May 31). Institutional portfolio management: A framework to improve institutional performance. *EduCause Review.* https://er.educause.edu/articles/2016/5/institutional-portfolio-management-a-framework-to-improve-institutional-performance

Chapter 4

Organizing for Student Learning

Overview: This chapter addresses the academic structural components necessary for any new academic program, including program outcomes, course learning outcomes, alignment with university outcomes, and assessment considerations. This chapter is important because new academic program proposals are often built from a blueprint of courses or outcomes that fit well together. That blueprint then becomes an active building process where course development, learning outcomes, and figuring out how to assess what students learn in the new program can be accomplished.

PRIORITIZING LEARNING IN NEW PROGRAM DEVELOPMENT

Revisiting a premise we laid out earlier in this book, the most effective and efficient way to build a new academic program is to create a strong proposal—one that details the importance of a new academic venture, why students will benefit from it, and how the new program complements the overall institutional goals. Thus, detailing and planning for the essential elements of a new academic program before implementation, shows careful consideration of potential challenges, needs, and processes that can be put in place to best set up a new program for success. Thinking holistically about a new program means considering the impact of a new program on the institution, the roles of people working within and around the new program, and the need to engage in various institutional processes that recruit, retain, and facilitate a student's time in a program.

In this chapter, we present some common universal structures and processes that inhabit many new academic program proposals. Within each area, the role of new program development is explored and potential issues for faculty leading the proposal and development process are discussed.

LEARNING OUTCOMES ALIGNMENT

Learning outcomes in a collegiate setting exist at a large scale, institution-wide level, a smaller, program-level, and an even more specific course level. The typical student in an institution of higher education engages in learning and activities that meet all these outcomes by the time of graduation. Institutional outcomes tend to be written to encompass the talents and skills of the entire student body—and what a typical graduate should know or be able to do, while program and course outcomes are focused more on disciplinary study and specific coursework a student completes within an academic program or major (figure 4.1).

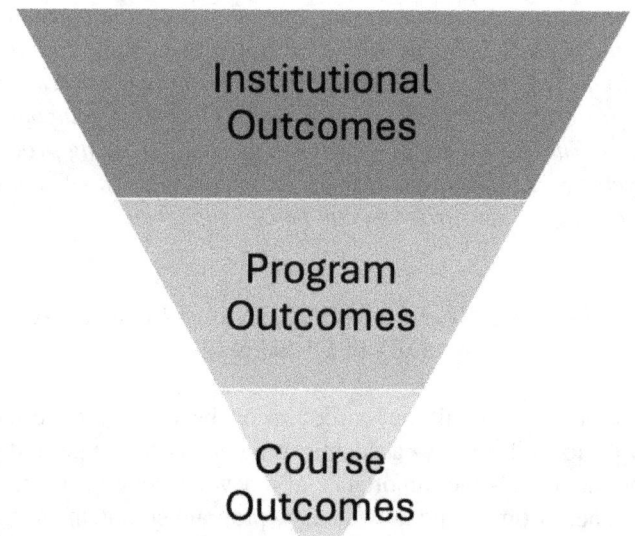

Figure 4.1   Typical Learning Outcomes Alignment

ALIGNMENT WITH INSTITUTIONAL OUTCOMES

Institutional outcomes are "knowledge, skills, abilities, and attitudes that students are expected to develop as a result of their overall experiences with any aspect of the college, including courses, programs, and student services" (Glendale Community College, 2024, para. 1). Institutional outcomes are typically measurable, specific, and inclusive of what all graduates of the institution can do upon graduation.

As an example, the University of Minnesota's university outcomes include generalized knowledge and skills that undergraduates receiving diplomas from the institution will have at the time of graduation. These include problem-solving, critical thinking, and communication. The University describes the outcome of problem-solving as the ability of a student to "identify, define, and solve problems" (para. 3). Critical thinking as an outcome expects that graduates "can locate and critically evaluate information," while communication establishes that graduates "can communicate effectively" (para. 3). Notice that institutional outcomes involve wide and generalized skills, knowledge, or abilities that can apply to any discipline throughout the institution. Specialized knowledge, then, is covered in program and course outcomes. With new program design and development, alignment with institutional outcomes is typically done after the program and its courses are developed. While it is important to keep in mind during the development phases, it is a bit easier to begin at the program level before considering how a program fits within a larger institutional framework.

CREATING PROGRAM OUTCOMES

Program outcomes are the knowledge, skills, abilities, and attitudes that students are expected to develop because of their experiences within a program or disciplinary area (major, course of studies, department, or similar entity). These statements are meant to guide a more specialized pursuit of knowledge that not only meets the institutional outcomes but also a more distinct set of skills or abilities that are found within the academic field of study.

Boston University's Provost's website (https://www.bu.edu/provost/files/2017/06/Creating-Learning-Outcomes-Stanford.pdf) suggests some thoughtful guidance on writing program and course outcomes—we share these below with some additional thoughts about application when designing a new academic program and an example using this sample program outcome:

Outcome A: "Students Will Know or Be Able to Use Effective Communication with Underserved Populations"

- Learning outcomes should be specific and well defined: this helps provide stability and structure to a new program. The more specific (measurable) and defined (explained), the better an audience seeking to learn the how and why of a new program will be.

- In Outcome A: students will be assessed on their ability to use effective communication skills specifically when working with underserved populations.
- Learning outcomes should be realistic: for new program development, think specifically about what can be done in the time allotted for the program. If a degree path is two years, design outcomes that can reasonably be achieved in that timeframe (not after graduation or once in an established career setting).
  - In Outcome A, it would be expected that during the program or course, students would learn about various communication techniques and, more specifically, which techniques are appropriate for the audience they are trying to reach (underserved populations).
- Learning outcomes should rely on active verbs in the future tense: for new program development, this means looking into the future and thinking about the skills, knowledge, and abilities that anyone completing the program will have.
  - In Outcome A, note the verb phrasing, "will know or be able to use" is written so that it is expected that students will acquire new skills that can then be practiced and measured during the time of the course or program.
- Learning outcomes should be framed in terms of the program instead of specific classes that the program offers: In terms of new program development, design outcomes that encompass the whole of learning in the program, whether that be a series of courses or an entire degree plan.
  - In Outcome A, students might learn communication techniques in several different courses. They may also learn the dynamics of working with underserved populations in a series of courses or units of study.
- There should be a sufficient number of learning outcomes: Boston University recommends no more than three to five learning outcomes. Fewer than three makes the assessment process limited in scope, while more than five can make the assessment process (what students have learned) arduous.
- Learning outcomes should align with the program's curriculum: For new programs, ensure that what graduating students need to know or be able to do is taught within the program's courses (whether under development or already developed).
- Learning outcomes should be simple and not compound: An extremely important point for new program development. The simpler the outcome, the easier it will be to assess whether students are learning and achieving the intended outcomes.

In Outcome A, it is clear that students will be focusing on the use of communication skills to reach an underserved population (not all populations, not all communication skills).

- Learning outcomes should focus on learning products and not the learning process. For new programs, consider the types of products that are appropriate for the field of study and integrate those into course development assessments.

(Boston University, n.d.)

A FORMULA FOR PROGRAM OUTCOME DESIGN

Simple is best. Thus, in order to write program or course outcomes that are specific and measurable, we have come to appreciate a formula suggested by the University of Missouri (2024). This formula for program outcome development follows a simple pattern:

Action Verb + Noun (+ Condition + Timescale)

Some examples of program learning outcomes for a leadership program might be:

- Students will analyze organizational behavior during the Covid-19 pandemic.
- Students will compare and contrast the leadership styles of a nonprofit agency.
- Students will utilize a strategic planning analysis tool to critique the working conditions of employees at a Fortune 500 company.

Program learning outcomes are important for any new program development in that they provide a structure for how the program fits within the larger institution, but also how graduates will have specific skills, knowledge, and abilities upon graduation—adding credibility to the substance of the program. In new program design, it is expected that program outcomes may be fluid and under development until a proposal has been formally approved or coursework has been developed and adopted by the institution. However, regarding a strong program proposal, the more specific and articulate program outcomes are laid out, the more cohesive the overall plan for program development can be.

CRAFTING COURSE LEARNING OUTCOMES

Course outcomes are the final layer of curricular design of new program elements and closely follow the same template for writing program learning outcomes. What differs, then, is that course learning outcomes pertain to a specific course or set of learning events. For example, course learning outcomes might be what students will know or be able to do after a semester-long course or seminar. Here are some possible course learning outcomes for a speech communications course:

By the end of Speech 501, students will know or be able to:

1. Utilize basic communication skills in a variety of real-life contexts
2. Critically analyze messages during conversations
3. Identify strategies for adapting a speech for a particular audience

Think about not only the approaches that will be used in teaching (student-centered, project-based learning, lectures, discussions), but also how you can realistically measure those pieces through assessments (formative or summative), assignments, student products, or processes within the course.

ENSURING OUTCOMES ENCOURAGE LEARNING

The art of writing program or course learning outcomes involves staying simple (not overwhelming the outcome with too many things to measure or verbs that do not match what students actually do within a program), yet also understanding how students can demonstrate the depth of their learning in different ways. Many new programs utilize Bloom's Taxonomy—a hierarchy of cognitive skills used in most classrooms. The framework builds in complexity of knowledge production, with the lowest levels of learning being based on recall or remembering information. The next level of complexity requires students to "understand" ideas or concepts, moving beyond just remembering to a deeper level of exploration. The next level moves to application, then to analyzing, then to evaluation, and finally, the top-tier of the most complex cognitive skills of "creating" or producing new information (figure 4.2).

Example: Consider a K–12 teacher education program where teachers are learning to design lesson plans for their science classrooms. Throughout the program, students may learn about lesson plan design, read different lesson plans, analyze lesson plans from various teachers, watch teachers teach using different lesson plans, and might even create their own lesson plans. Thus, students can demonstrate learning at many different levels from simple to the most complex:

Being able to identify the parts of a lesson plan (remember)
Explaining the parts of a lesson plan (understand)
Using a lesson plan template to design a lesson of their own (apply)
Comparing and contrasting a lesson plan to teach a specific unit (analyze)

Organizing for Student Learning 63

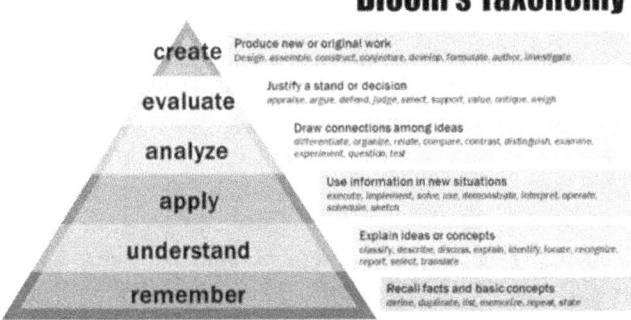

Figure 4.2 Bloom's Taxonomy to Create Meaningful Course and Program Outcomes

Critiquing lesson plans designed by students in the class (evaluate)
Design a new lesson plan for a unit of study (create)

Again, with new program development, it is important to design learning in a scaffolded manner, one which builds on prior learning to strengthen students' understanding of the discipline. Within each course, and throughout the program, students should have the chance to practice learning at all levels of Bloom's Taxonomy, with the higher levels showing a more developed understanding of the application of learning.

ASSESSMENT

Assessment, or measuring and understanding what students learn at the end of a course or program, is a process embedded in nearly every institution. While the approaches might be different (measuring program outcomes versus institutional outcomes), the goal is the same: to better recognize the learning that is taking place and the gaps that need to be filled. From the proposal stage, this might be a bit ambiguous or remain in "draft" mode for a while, which is completely appropriate. Once courses are built and teaching and learning take place, the ways to gather information about that learning become clearer.

Santa Clara University uses a cyclical process of evaluation, gathering data, evaluating that data, and then using it to improve teaching practices and processes. They identify five unique steps: (1) define the mission and goals; (2) articulate student learning outcomes; (3) align those learning outcomes with the experiences that students have within a course or program; (4) identify an appropriate assessment method and gather data on those outcomes; and (5) interpret and use the results to inform future practices (Santa Clara

University, 2024, para. 1). Assessment, then, is never-ending, so it is wise to clearly understand the need for clear student outcomes, the ways those can be measured, and how that information can create better practices overall.

Within assessment, we've met many faculty who are a bit nervous about their own expertise in methodology—whether it be in collecting quantitative data from student surveys or analyzing qualitative data for relevant themes. What we've found is that because this is a universal process, it is generally not one done alone. Faculty are able to work together to analyze data, to understand emerging themes, or to design recommended next steps. Your own methodological expertise will be useful, but do not rely on that as the only way to assess student learning—be open to other means of gathering data and understanding how learning is happening, and when you need help, turn to your colleagues who have expertise in other areas to strengthen your work.

ACCREDITATION

Accreditation is an extremely important asset for any institution of higher education. New programs must align with and fit in with already established regional accrediting organizations that ensure institutions are offering high-quality education, building improvement strategies, being accountable for their processes, and promoting student learning. It is important to note that regional accrediting agencies evaluate the entirety of an institution, not a specific discipline, college, or program within the body. A list of regional accrediting agencies can be found at https://www.chea.org/regional-accrediting-organizations.

In certain disciplines, course or program outcomes may be suggested or required by an accrediting organization. It is important to be aware of any organization from which the new program will need accreditation, whether at inception or in the future. Take, for example, leading a new master's degree in public health. The accrediting body for that program would be the Council on Education for Public Health (https://ceph.org/). Having the CEPH accreditation is an indication that the program has gone through an outside review process by professionals and experts in the field of study, and that graduates from those programs are able to identify, prevent, and solve a series of public health issues. The accreditation might be something that potential students seek when comparing which programs to consider enrolling in and also might impact the likelihood of their potential employment.

Some examples of accreditation bodies and standards include

Council for Higher Education Accreditation
https://www.chea.org/regional-accrediting-organizations

CACREP: https://www.cacrep.org/
Nursing: https://www.aacnnursing.org/ccne-accreditation
https://www.acenursing.org
Medical: MD and DO have different accreditors
https://accredmed.org/standards/
https://lcme.org/directory/
https://www.acgme.org
Pharmacy: https://www.acpe-accredit.org/continuing-education-provider-accreditation/
Teacher Preparation (K–12 Education):
http://www.caepnet.org/
https://www.chea.org/national-council-accreditation-teacher-education
*State licensure requirements
Social Work: https://www.cswe.org/accreditation/
Engineering: https://www.abet.org/
*This organization accredits programs in dozens of countries in engineering and computer science.

Accreditation requirements vary across fields and disciplines but should be identified and planned for within the program development process. Accreditation is not always a guarantee, and it is possible that a program will enroll students and then face a situation where accreditation is delayed or denied. The only way to prepare to lessen this potential is through careful planning, a thorough understanding of the accreditation process and the resources needed to complete it, and support from the institution that requirements to meet accreditation will be supported through necessary resources, documentation, and processes.

QUESTIONS FOR YOUR REFLECTION

1. As you've read through the various aspects of program building here, what processes do you feel confident about, and where do you still have lingering concerns? How might you find some resources to help with those concerns?
2. Identify your strengths within the areas explored in this chapter. Are you a master of aligning outcomes with assignments that measure those outcomes? How can you utilize those strengths to amplify a new program proposal?
3. Locate your institutional assessment practices, processes, and documents (generally found on the institutional website). Where are the resources within the institution to help faculty better understand these

processes? Are there development opportunities? Where would you go to learn more about all of this?
4. Who manages the assessment within your institution? Are there different layers of management within colleges, departments, or programs? What do these people do, and how do they articulate the assessment priorities of the institution?
5. How do the outcomes for learning align with your institution's mission, vision, and strategic plan? Can clear pathways be drawn from what students are learning to the larger aspirations of the institution?

Part II

LEADING NEW ACADEMIC PROGRAMS IN HIGHER EDUCATION

Chapter 5

Leaning into Leadership

Overview: Building a new academic program, in any discipline, institution, or program requires a shift from the traditional faculty role to a leadership stance—and not always with the language of a new contract, delineations of expectations, or even measurable performance outcomes. Many leaders of new academic programs find themselves entrenched in processes they never had to know as a faculty member—from enrollment to marketing to alumni relations. Additionally, whether assigned as a formal leadership position or not, creating and advocating for a new program is a leadership process, one that requires strategic planning, insightful consideration of audiences, and deliberate reflection. This chapter explains how you can embrace your role as a leader, whether it be an expected or unexpected development in your academic career.

HOW'D YOU GET HERE ANYWAY?

One thing that has surprised us in our decade as Program Directors of our own new academic programs was the origin stories of our colleagues at other institutions across the country. At the time we began building our respective programs, we were both new faculty members at our respective institutions who apparently showed the talent or bandwidth to be viable candidates to lead a new program. We'd both had leadership positions in other employment in the past, so it wasn't a stretch to shift us from our academic teaching roles to more administrative duties, but it was also something that our colleagues would express confusion about and/or lack of interest in learning themselves.

How you got here, to the point of reading this book, is probably more about who you are as an employee, colleague, and person. You've shown a spark of innovation, flexibility, or adeptness at thinking about education in different ways. Additionally, somewhere, you've shown some leadership capacity. We've talked to new academic program leaders who were hired specifically to build a program from scratch, while others were handed a fully vetted new program proposal and told to "make it happen." One program director told us that he was named as a new academic program leader before he even had a chance to say no to the position, while another shared that she knew that creating a new program was the only way her fledgling department would survive upcoming budget cuts.

The problem with shifting academic teaching or research faculty into administrative roles is a common one: lack of training. It's not unusual for department chairs, associate deans, or provosts to have no formal leadership training. Their training tends to be solely within their academic discipline, focusing on publishing, teaching, and research. Thus, the expectation that even the most talented faculty member can easily lead a program is a mismatch of skills. Some academics are poorly suited for leadership, while others thrive in the environment.

LEADERSHIP 101 FOR NEW ACADEMIC PROGRAM LEADERS

Capturing all the leadership skills, attributes, and talents needed to successfully lead a new academic program is an impossible task—particularly knowing that you are probably balancing several roles at once. You may be teaching classes, serving on campus committees, or embedded in research activities. Your time is limited and valuable, and adding formal leadership training onto your plate while you learn how to lead a new academic program is usually not possible. We've compiled a list of five essential leadership traits that, from our experiences, new academic program leaders should prepare to engage with as they build new avenues to learning at their institutions.

(a) Embracing a growth mindset: Taking the reins of a new academic program, whether it be at inception or implementation, is a process of trial and error. That is, even the best-articulated proposals still face challenges when putting pieces in place. Courses may not be built as easily as anticipated, faculty recruitment may not go seamlessly, or working with other facets of the institution may prove to be challenging. This is where embracing a growth mindset is integral for any new academic program leader. Studied by psychologist and author Carol Dweck, a growth mindset "thrives on challenges" and accepts that learning is a process that can be acquired through mentoring, practice, and failure

(Dweck, 2019, para. 4). Most new academic program leaders embrace the unknown in building a new program—the instability of finances, the muddiness of building course content, or the foggy nature of just how and where new students originate. This doesn't impede the new academic program leader, and rather than deter them from progress, it spurs them into asking questions, seeking advice from others, and studying programs that have successfully found a place within an institution.

(b) Willingness to collaborate: Collaboration, or the willingness to work with, for, and among others, is important for any new program leader. If you are coming from a traditional faculty role, you may be used to doing a lot of things on your own—from managing your own courses to engaging in research that you design. Conceptualizing and building a new academic program will require collaboration with others across your institution—from the business side to the marketing side to the admissions side. In all, these are areas that traditional faculty have little to no interaction with when working in teaching or research roles, yet they are a necessity when building a new academic program in that the program leader must learn how to identify the best methods of finding students, ways that institutional messaging can reach those students, and thoughtful approaches to engage students and alumni. In this, you may find that the "other" institutional entities are less than willing to teach you as you go. Thus, when you approach the admissions department with questions about how to build a student application, you may be met with resistance or annoyance. Continue to push for collaboration. Approach each relationship with care, in a way that respects the workload of others but that is also not demanding.

(c) Adapting to the unknown: There are many aspects of change that leading a new academic program will cause. The most prominent will most likely be in your daily job duties—whether you keep your prior position and add this task on, or whether you shift entirely to administrative or program leadership. When you are building a program, there is no precedent to rely on. There are no set or established rules to say, "we've always done it this way," and there are times when the answers to problems are not clear. Additionally, issues may arise that you've never had to address before (how does a student access financial aid? What are our policies for taking a leave of absence?) You may find that your institution has rigorous policies in place, and you struggle to figure out if the new program fits within those parameters, or you may find that your institution is very open to new processes and procedures, meaning that what you are building will build a path for other programs in the future.

(d) Asking meaningful questions: There is never a lack of questions to ask a new academic program leader. Whether it be how, why, when, or who to go to for questions, it is better to become known as someone asking a lot of questions than assuming the incorrect answers. This means you will have to reach out beyond your usual set of colleagues to visit those parts of the institution that you may not have ever communicated with before. It may mean asking potential students why they would attend your institution above others, or it may be asking faculty how they feel best supported on their own professional growth paths. Asking questions is not a sign of poor leadership. It is a sign of inquisitive, intelligent pursuit of how best to build something worthwhile.

(e) Promoting student achievement and faculty growth: In program leadership, it can be easy to get caught up in the signatures that need to be obtained or the administrative meetings that you suddenly find yourself among. However, one thing should always be clear in your work: your job as a new academic program leader is to promote student achievement and faculty growth. So, as you sit in meetings about budget cuts or enrollment decisions, always ask yourself how the decisions in front of you will impact the ability of students in the program to learn and the faculty in your program to thrive as academics.

These recommended leadership traits are not exclusive to what will make or break you as a new academic program leader. You bring a unique set of skills, background knowledge, talents, and abilities that help build your reputation as a new academic program leader. You will find challenges where others will not, and you will find some processes easier than others to conquer—thus the need for adaptability and flexibility in embracing the fact that nothing you are doing will always go as planned.

FIGURING OUT HOW YOU LEAD

Because new academic program leaders often come from a disciplinary background, it's possible that you have no idea what type of leader you are. You've experienced different types of leadership within your institution and can probably point out the strengths and weaknesses of various leaders across your campus. But how can you figure out how you lead best? In addition to formal leadership training programs, you might find some common leadership assessment tools useful in your search to articulate your leadership style. These are tests you can take in your own time and evaluate yourself, that might include assessments like CliftonStrengths, the Myers-Briggs Personality Indicator, or the Enneagram Personality Assessment. Any leadership style assessment can provide information about how you lead and how that can impact those around you.

Your leadership style is really what you want to understand most, as that is not only guides how and why you make the decisions that you do but also can help you understand where you may have conflicts with your colleagues. Leadership styles tend to fall into one of several categories: authoritarian, democratic, or laissez-faire. Each has pros and cons, and within leading a new academic program, it may be necessary to shift from your dominant style to another in order to fit the situation (this is called situational leadership). Briefly, these three main styles of leadership are described as:

- Authoritarian: This style of leadership tends to be controlling and directive. Northouse (2019) described authoritarian leaders as having a "need to control followers and what they do" (Northouse, 2019, p. 62), adding that "these leaders are in charge, exert influence and control".
- Democratic: This style of leadership is less controlling and more collective in its work with followers. Democratic leaders give suggestions, help followers reach professional goals, and utilize communication as a means of finding consensus.
- Laissez-faire: This style of leadership is labeled by Northouse as "non-leadership" (Northouse, 2019, p. 64). A laissez-faire leader is hands-off, interacts very seldom with followers, and may appear disinterested or unengaged. It can be hard to work under a laissez-faire leader due to their lack of direction, but it can also work quite well for someone who is highly independent and needs little direction or oversight.

Regardless of where you fall on the leadership spectrum, or what your leadership style or personality type is, there is no wrong answer. That is, successful leaders can be found within every style and type. What makes these leaders successful is that they make efforts to understand how they lead, how that impacts others, and how they may need to adapt their approach to reach their intended outcomes. This really requires flexibility, intuitiveness, and reflection to see that you are not working in a silo, but working among and with others who may be motivated or may work in very different ways than you. When you can articulate how you lead, the style you lead with primarily, and how you can adjust that style to adapt to the needs of others, your leadership capacity will be clearly identifiable.

LEADERSHIP MENTORS

Understanding how and why you lead the way that you do is a great starting point for a new academic program leader, regardless of your leadership experience or time in position. However, one practice that strengthens your leadership capacity is to find a mentor or mentors who can provide honest feedback and insights into your work and approach to your role within the new program. Good mentors can be hard to find, so you want to be on the lookout not only within your institution but at colleagues who may be in similar roles at other institutions or in the experiences of those who have led a new academic program in an entirely different discipline. Seek out someone who is willing to mentor you, who has the capacity and time to meet with you frequently (we suggest at least twice a semester), and who is willing to challenge some of your more problematic habits or traits. As you work in leadership, you may find yourself thinking that you can learn it all on your own or that you've learned enough that you simply don't need a leadership mentor. However, mentors can do several things for us, including reducing the feelings of isolation that often accompany leadership roles, sharing their own lived experiences, providing advice from someone who has been in the same role, and expanding your professional network (Elliott, 2023).

FAILURE WITHIN LEADERSHIP

No leadership journey is without trials or tribulations. Even the best leaders fail—and failure, it seems, is the "prerequisite for invention" (Farson & Keyes, 2002, para. 1). We tend to accept that failure happens within our institutions—we've been part of plans that fell apart or initiatives that did not fully come to fruition—but personal failure is a different aspect of leadership. Farson and Keyes describe this human tendency, writing, "Everyone hates to fail. We assume, rationally or not, that we'll suffer embarrassment and a loss of esteem and stature. And nowhere is the fear of failure more intense and debilitating than in the competitive world of business, where a mistake can mean losing a bonus, a promotion, or even a job" (para. 3). Higher education is business, and failure can be as daunting there as in any business setting.

Rather than fear failure, new academic program leaders need to embrace failure—not in a haphazard or careless way, but in a way that shows that failure can lead to better understanding, growth, and maturity. Failing allows for things to be redone or rebuilt and for learning to take place. Farson and Keyes suggest questions that "failure-tolerant" leaders ask in the face of failure—we've adapted these to the setting of leading a new academic program (para. 8). These might include questions such as:

- Was the new academic program designed purposefully?
- Could the failure have been prevented with more thorough research, collaboration, or consultation?

- Was a collaborative process utilized in building the new academic program, and were participants in the design and implementation process fully on board and invested in the program's success?
- Are the initial goals of the new academic program consistent over time? Are they achievable and measurable?
- Were anticipated risks, costs, and timing accurate?
- Were mistakes in planning or implementation repeated multiple times? (para. 8)

As a new academic program leader, you will fail. But you will also fail if you continue your work as a teaching or research faculty member or if you quit your job and move to an entirely new industry. Failure is present in all aspects of our lives, including our professional lives, so we must learn to embrace failure and the opportunities it presents to learn and grow.

Professional Growth

As new academic program leaders, we've come to recognize that our own professional growth often lands last on our to-do list during the first few years of building a new program. Priorities become writing courses, designing assessments, and managing student and faculty issues. However, it is essential that any new academic program leader, regardless of time spent in academia, continue a professional growth trajectory. In this, it might mean a shift from your usual routes of professional presentations or conferences within your discipline to attending leadership conferences, higher education events, or even learning events for academic leaders. Target your professional learning in three areas: (a) gaining a better understanding of your own leadership abilities; (b) navigating the changing landscape of higher education; and (c) self-care strategies for leaders in higher education.

PRIORITIZING SELF-CARE

Why does a new academic program leader need to prioritize self-care? It's essential to ensure that you have the energy, mental fortitude, and longevity to do your job well. In today's higher education institutions, nearly 63 percent of faculty report feeling burned out because of their job (Vyletel, 2023). This is due to a variety of factors, including increasing workloads, adapting to changing processes and practices, lack of recognition, and minimal input into decision-making (American Psychological Association, 2024).

The pressure on faculty and academic leaders continues to rise as budgets tighten, enrollments decline, and the needs of students evolve. One constant through all of this is that no one will prioritize your own care except for you. It is vitally important to establish a manageable workload, to define boundaries between your work and personal life, and to prioritize what is important and what can wait. As a new academic program leader, you may find yourself pulled in multiple directions at once—the admissions department needs information for an application, the accreditation report is due next week, and you are a week late preparing next year's budget. The pressures will not be the same or predictable, but when you put yourself first—caring for your mental, physical, and emotional well-being—you strengthen your leadership capacity.

QUESTIONS FOR YOUR REFLECTION

1. What kind of leader do you hope to be as you lead a new academic program? How will you know if you've achieved that?
2. Think about the different types of leaders you've worked with throughout your career. What made the good ones exceptional, and what made the weaker ones challenging?
3. Take some time to discover your own leadership style. How can that style be an advantage or disadvantage when leading a new academic program?
4. What is your tolerance for failure? How can you embrace failure as a learning opportunity?
5. What are three things you can do to promote your own well-being and self-care during the busiest times of the academic year?

Chapter 6

Leading Students in a New Academic Program

Overview: The current climate for new academic program development often focuses on the debate between face-to-face, hybrid, and online learning. While the mode of delivery is important, so, too, is recognizing the changing faces and needs of students who will be the future of the program. Effective new academic program leaders will anticipate the unique opportunities present in adult learning theories, educating first-generation students, adults returning to the classroom after a period of absence, and students from a wide variety of social and economic backgrounds. Key questions include: who are your students (first-gen, military, transfer, adult/working, running start, etc.) and what needs do those students have? In addition, are you serving students that already exist in your community, or are you creating programs to pull in and attract new students?

Regardless of your program area, understanding student populations is important as the new academic program leader. Does your proposed program serve traditional undergraduate students, nontraditional undergraduate students, or graduate students? Are your students predominantly local or from a wider geographic area? What are their demographics? How do each of these considerations affect the design of your program? In a post-pandemic higher education environment, there is no longer a question about modality. Faculty and programs must consider the pros and cons of face-to-face, hybrid, and synchronous/asynchronous online modalities. This chapter will focus on leading the people who are the lifeblood of your program: the students.

In the first half of this book, we posed questions for you to consider about the types, how many, and overall profile of potential students for your new academic program. Now, consider that applications have been processed, enrollment is complete, and students are ready to take classes in the program.

As a program leader, your job of tending to student needs is not done once admissions are complete—rather, your job becomes more intense, necessary, and proactive in ensuring students are participating in a quality educational program while also working hard to meet the discipline or industry standards for the disciplinary area.

WHO ARE THE STUDENTS THAT WE SERVE?

Every institution of higher education has had to become more astute in recognizing the unique types of students that are drawn to their programs. Depending on location, area of expertise, cost, or ease of access, some institutions are able to survive as traditional undergraduate institutions with only face-to-face classes. Other institutions have shifted to more accessible options, including online learning, options for full-time employed adults, or students returning to school several years after their first attempt.

Higher education is an incredibly diverse environment, and the demographic breakdown of students can be vastly different depending on your location and institutional type. When considering a new academic program, one of the key areas for analysis is student demographics. In order to leverage your new program for success, it should be designed to meet current and future student needs. Many of these needs are related to their identity and demographic profile. These student characteristics and the impact those characteristics have on students' academic experiences are of utmost importance when seeking to retain and graduate students.

The National Student Clearinghouse® Research Center™ reported that over 15 million undergraduate students and nearly 3 million graduate students were enrolled in 2023–2024 in all types of educational institutions across the United States (including community colleges, graduate programs, professional degree programs, and associate degree programs). Within these populations, there were several subgroups or characteristics of students that are relevant to a new academic program leader because their learning needs may differ from those of traditional undergraduate students (Schmerle, 2024). Consider these subgroups and their unique needs here:

Sex and gender: The number of female college students slightly outnumbers male college students. In spring 2024, the National Clearinghouse reported around 8 million female undergraduate students in comparison to about 5 million male undergraduates. In graduate schools, the numbers were a bit more even, with female graduate students slightly outnumbering male graduate students. While more women are present in programs than in years past, women still face significant issues once enrolled in higher education. Specifically, there are fewer women faculty teaching in higher education (men, in fact, nearly double the number of women faculty). Women tend to acquire more student loan debt than men, women tend to face more mental health challenges during college than men, and when women graduate, their salaries are not always comparable to men's salaries in the same industries (Welding, 2023).

Considerations for new academic program leaders: Pay careful attention to the gender balance in your program, both among your students and your faculty members. Ensure that all students have access to campus services like counseling and financial information. Advocate for equity in women's pay within your field of study.

Adult learners: In 2023–2024, over 5 million adult learners (those twenty-five5 years of age and over) were studying in undergraduate and graduate programs throughout the United States. Adult learners originate from many different backgrounds—some are returning to school after having completed some courses during their traditional-age learning years. Others are entering college for the first time after working professionally or raising a family, while others are pursuing graduate degrees or professional degrees. Teaching adult learners is more about facilitation than knowledge transfer. New academic program leaders should know the adult learning theory, andragogy, espoused by Malcolm Knowles. Andragogy is a proposed set of assumptions that faculty should use when teaching adult learners. These include

- Adults have a need to know.
- Adults are self-directed.
- Adults draw upon their lived experiences.
- Adults have a readiness to learn.
- An adult's orientation to learning is life-centered.
- Adults are driven by a motivation to learn (Knowles, 1990).

Adult learners need to see practical applications for what they are learning. Rather than being overwhelmed with theory or constructs of ideas, adult learners want to know how what they are learning applies in real life. They want to relate learning to what they've learned in their own experiences, and they have a strong desire to learn.

Considerations for new academic program leaders: Adult learners are present in every level of college education, so regardless of the design of the new academic program you are leading, you should be prepared to work with adult learners. Knowing the principles of why adult learners learn differently can help you understand why they may be asking for professional practice experiences, for direct applications of learning to real-world events, or for the expectation that a new academic program will be ready to deliver what is promised upon graduation.

Military veterans: In 2017, there were around 900,000 veterans attending school utilizing VA benefits. The Veterans Administration explored some unique characteristics these students face, including a high percentage of male versus female students, most of them being first-generation college students, nontraditional aged students, and students with families of their own to care for (US Dept of Veterans Affairs, n.d.).

Considerations for new academic program leaders: Students with military experience often bring a wealth of background knowledge and lived experiences to the classroom. However, they often need to work with campus offices that deal specifically with Military and Veteran Affairs, where they can gain specialized advice on how to utilize their military benefits, any specific regulations regarding the types of programs in which they can enroll, and any time limits they have for their course of study. It's also possible that these students may be involved in active duty, deployed overseas, or face attendance challenges because of their service duties. As a new academic program leader, you should not only know who works in your Military and Veteran Affairs office, but also how students can access the personnel within that office when their needs call for specific paperwork, signatures, or scholarship information.

First-generation students: Another profile of students in today's college campuses are first-generation students, or individuals whose parents did not graduate from college (Center for First-Generation, 2020). In 2020, 54 percent of undergraduate students in the United States identified as first-generation. These students may face hurdles accessing financial aid, understanding the complex nature of processes within a college campus, or even locating the proper resources to assist with academic, financial, or personal concerns.

Considerations for the new academic program leader: First-generation college students make up over half the undergraduate population and can be found throughout graduate schools and professional schools as well. These students may come from families with a lower parental income. Additionally, they may lack knowledge of the "hidden curriculum" of higher education—that is, a working understanding of higher education and its typical processes or traditions that a student whose parent attended college may possess and share with them (Chronicle Intelligence, 2024, para. 8). First-generation students also tend to be older, may be going to school while working, and may have families of their own to support (Center for First-Generation, 2020).

Students with disabilities: Students with accessibility challenges study at every college campus. Unlike the K–12 education system, college students (both undergraduate and graduate) must self-advocate to receive equitable learning opportunities. Whether it be for a permanent or temporary disability, eligible students are protected by Section 504 of the Rehabilitation Act of 1973, the Americans with Disabilities Act, and the ADA Amendments Act of 2008. These protections include reasonable accommodations and services that may not be provided to all students. Identified students must provide documentation of their disability and must work with their campus accessibility office to ensure that faculty are aware of and agreeable to accommodations or needs that a student may have during a course.

Considerations for the new academic program leader: Student disabilities should not preclude students from entering any academic program. However, as a new academic program leader, it may be helpful to become familiar with the staff at the institution's accessibility office. Over time, you may find the need to direct students to that office to gain formal documentation of a necessary accommodation or to understand how a requested accommodation may need to be adjusted to fit your content area.

Part-time students: Part-time students can be found attending all types of colleges and universities, and they may be part-time for a variety of reasons: financial challenges, family obligations, access to coursework, or even simply choosing to attend school less than full-time.

Considerations for the new academic program leader: Attending part-time may allow students to balance multiple obligations, but it may also interfere with the typical progression of coursework, graduating within an anticipated standard time frame, or having access to coursework that is only offered sporadically—all of which are programmatic issues and not caused by a lack of student talent or ambition. If you are leading a graduate degree or a degree that is aimed at enrolling working adults, these students may need or prefer courses online, offered in the evening, or the opportunity to access campus resources during nontraditional working hours. Additionally, students who attend college part-time face challenges in that their financial aid is prorated, their access to courses may be limited, and they may face a constant balance of work, school, and family obligations. If nothing else, recognizing that these students are balancing priorities and may be progressing toward their degree at a different pace than expected of full-time students should be a given.

International students: International students make up about 5 percent of the undergraduate population and 20 percent of the graduate population in US colleges and universities (Higher Ed Immigration, 2024). These students can attend colleges with an F-1 visa, which is issued by the US Department of

State. The US Department of Homeland Security governs the actions of international students once they enter the country's borders, so the complexities of managing this can be quite cumbersome for someone new to the country. Most international students will not qualify for state or federal financial aid, so there can be significant financial issues for students who lack funding or have unstable funding resources.

Considerations for the new academic program leader: International students and their ability to live in the United States are governed by the federal government and its policies. Students often need visas or other paperwork that permit them to live in the United States for a specific amount of time to complete their program of study. You need to understand whether your institution is permitted to accept international students, who deals with the visa paperwork, and where international students can receive resources while on campus. Over time, these students may require proof of enrollment or attendance, which you may be asked to provide and verify.

Students as caretakers: Caretaking can take many forms in a college student's life today. From caring for young children, elderly or ailing parents, or their own health or wellness challenges, it is not uncommon to work with students who are balancing multiple roles in their personal lives. Forbes.com contributor Edward Conroy reported that knowing the exact needs of students who are also parents can be hard to determine because not a lot of data is collected regarding this particular group. However, some states are seeing an uptick in the need for data collection and specific policies and legislation that support students attending college and balancing the needs of their own children and families.

Considerations for the new academic program leader: The needs of students who are caretaking—in any form—will be varied and unique. A student caring for a toddler may face different personal demands than one parenting their own college student. Additionally, a student caring for a dying parent may have different needs than a student caring for a spouse with a long-term illness. These students may need flexibility with scheduling, attendance requirements, due dates, or field experiences.

Immigrant students: As of 2021, around 2 percent of college students in the United States were undocumented immigrants (American Immigration Council, 2023). In all, the United States is home to about 408,000 undocumented students (Higher Ed Immigration Portal, 2024). One recent group to see a surge in college attendance were DACA-eligible students (Deferred Action for Childhood Arrivals). DACA students are undocumented individuals who arrived as children prior to 2007 and who grew up in American schools. As of the time of this publication, only students who entered the United States prior to 2007 receive DACA protections, so as students born in 2008 and beyond begin to enter college, DACA protections may not be available. While it is not illegal for undocumented students to apply for or attend college in the United States, significant barriers can cause hesitation in applying to or affording higher education, including the lack of documentation or access to federal or state financial aid opportunities.

Considerations for new academic program leaders: Immigrant students, whether documented or not, must comply with institutional requirements. Some face difficulties accessing in-state tuition, state-based financial aid, obtaining a driver's license, or even providing necessary background information for professional licensure requirements. Additionally, even if admitted to an institution, there may be further challenges gaining certification or licensure within professional groups or bodies that are necessary for some career positions, like law or health care.

WHERE DO YOU FIND KEY STUDENT DEMOGRAPHICS DATA?

Understanding your institution's student demographics may mean digging through several different websites and resources to best understand who attends your institution and what their particular background details may be. A few general resources that help with new program implementation might be:

- The IPEDS System (Integrated Postsecondary Education Data System). A publicly available data system; this site allows for custom searches for different groups of students, their populations at institutions, and other pertinent resources. See more here: https://nces.ed.gov/ipeds/use-the-data
- Most institutions of higher education promote the diversity of their student population on their school's website—whether it be on an admissions information page or on an institutional research page.
- The Education Data Initiative hosts a thorough website that provides easy access to college enrollment and student demographics figures (Hanson, 2024).

Understanding the demographics at your institution is one piece of the puzzle when pursuing the launch of a new academic program. It may be that the new academic program is designed to draw a new, previously untapped population of students into the institution (adult learners, virtual learners, learners with a specific expertise). Additionally, it is important to decipher how your targeted students can fit in with existing demographics and where there might be opportunities to build additional resources or strengthen diversity among staff in order to best meet the needs of all students.

HIGH-IMPACT PRACTICES

High-impact practices set forth in 2007 by the American Association of Colleges and Universities (AAC&U) suggest that all students throughout their educational careers should participate in engaging educational processes and structures that promote learning, achievement, and advancement for all. The learning outcomes included "knowledge of human cultures and the physical and natural world, intellectual and practical skills, personal and social responsibility, and integrative learning (National Leadership Council for Liberal Education & America's Promise 2007, p. 3). Looking more closely at these student outcomes, new academic programs are poised to begin high-impact practices in place—if done so purposefully and with the implementation of these in mind.

To engage with high-impact practices, new academic program leaders should carefully consider how knowledge is constructed within the new program discipline, what practical skills students gain, how personal and social responsibility might be cultivated, and how learning can be achieved in new and innovative ways. By doing so, not only will students be engaged in their learning, but they will also be prepared for the challenges and opportunities that a rapidly changing world can present throughout their careers.

HOW DO YOU USE THIS INFORMATION TO LEAD A NEW ACADEMIC PROGRAM?

Until those first student applications arrive and you've admitted a cohort of students into a new academic program, much of the planning for students is anticipatory at best. When students arrive, more strategic decisions can be made about how the demographics or needs of the students within the new academic program may differ or may promote additional diversity across campus. However, there are some universal considerations that any new academic program leader should put in place for any students venturing into a new academic program. We pose these as three questions:

(a). Are you designing a program that is developmentally appropriate for your target students? Think about the necessary preparation that students need in order to do well in the new academic program. How can you ensure that their learning needs are met, that they have the proper background to do well in their courses, and that the pacing of their courses is appropriate for their professional preparation?

(b). Are you designing a program that promotes a sense of belonging for your students? Belonging, as a construct, is important for students to feel like they are part of a campus and invested in their learning. Your program design, course layout, academic activities, and assessment practices should promote a community of learning where students feel engaged, challenged, and like their place in each course matters. Not only will this promote stronger relationships among faculty and students, but it will also increase the likelihood that students stay to complete a program in full.

(c) Have you carefully recognized the academic preparation and technological preparation of your students? Regardless of their demographics, where might your target students lack knowledge of current technology necessary to do well in classes? What supports need to be in place to onboard students, considering their prior preparation?

QUESTIONS FOR YOUR REFLECTION

1. Who are your target students? How do those students fit or not fit within the current demographics of your institution?
2. How might you promote diversity among your students?
3. What can you do, as a new academic program leader, to foster inclusion and belonging among students?
4. How will you communicate with students about the new program? What will be your plan for regular communications or ways to share new explorations, opportunities, or career possibilities?
5. What do you prioritize in your communication with students? Professionalism? Timeliness? Accuracy? Responsiveness? How will you meet these various expectations, knowing the demands on your time?
6. How will students know that you are accessible to them with issues or questions about the new program?
7. How can you ensure high-impact practices are present in the new academic program? What evidence will you look for to ensure these are implemented with fidelity?

Chapter 7

Preparing to Lead Faculty

Overview: Faculty considerations are another often overlooked facet in new academic program development. That is, new programs are sometimes launched without clear hiring plans (or none at all), or with the assumption that added workload for existing faculty will occur without complaint. This chapter provides constructive advice on how to advocate for the proper allotment of faculty, how to navigate political issues like sharing faculty across campus divisions, learning how to mentor others, and the importance of delegation.

THE IMPORTANCE OF FACULTY

Faculty, of course, are an integral part of any new academic proposal—whether it be in proposal or implementation stages. Faculty are the key personnel who design content, deliver instruction, and assess student work. It is important to not only ensure that a new academic program has qualified faculty, but also appropriate bandwidth to work on pieces that are unique to developing a new academic program. This might include new course design, curriculum alignment, meeting with institution stakeholders, building assessment processes, and/or developing processes and policies within the program. Already established programs have these pieces in place, which is why it is especially important to allot time and responsibilities specifically to doing pieces that other programs do not have to do in a fully implemented stage.

As faculty who have written, developed, implemented, and assessed new academic programs, we can attest to the unexpected hurdles, the necessity to build campus-wide relationships, requests for documentation, and the dedicated time needed to build not only a new program framework but the pieces that make the program function daily. Processes like designing admission requirements, ensuring aligned marketing messaging, and building a budget are not typical faculty responsibilities—and most of us have little to no training in these areas. Thus, we learned as we went—we talked to marketing experts who could help us craft just the right words to optimize when a potential student does a Google search for a program, we reviewed dozens of admissions application processes to design the best fit for the program at our institution, and we attended meeting after meeting to explain the need, design, and outlook for the new program.

Most new academic proposals begin with one faculty lead or a small group of program development experts. These initial groupings are tasked with working through any required institutional proposal paperwork, processes, or requirements. Additionally, much time is spent making the case for the new academic program in ways aside from financial or employment demands. St. Bonaventure University in New York lists a multitude of questions for new program developers (some we've covered in other chapters in this book), but we share these here to demonstrate the vast breadth of topics that faculty need to be able to manage during new program development and implementation. These questions include

- Is the proposed program consistent with and supportive of the mission and strategic direction of the university?
- Can the proposed program be delivered with sufficient academic quality?
- Is the proposed program free from duplication or competition with a current or planned program within the university? If not, to what extent is it expected that enrollments in this program will decrease enrollments in one or more existing programs, or otherwise compete with existing program(s) for resources?
- Does the proposed program have characteristics that are distinctive from similar programs offered by the competition? (St. Bonaventure, 2012).

Faculty serve as the champions of a new academic program. Whether you serve as the program designer, director, associate director, or teaching faculty, your work will shape the strength and future of the program. In this, it's important to understand that many of the tasks that you are facing are things you have never done before, that you may do wrong, or that you may need to ask for help to fully complete. This is one of the most challenging and invigorating things about building a new academic program—learning something new, engaging in new and different conversations, and forging relationships to establish something unique at your institution. Can it be frustrating? Sure. Can it also awaken that natural academic drive you possess to innovate, create, and build something? Absolutely!

ESTIMATING FACULTY NEEDS WITHIN A NEW ACADEMIC PROGRAM

Generally, new academic programs do not begin with a fully lined department of faculty, support staff, and administrators. More typically, new academic programs start with one or two faculty members (depending on student enrollment, accreditation requirements, or other considerations), and as the program grows, so, too, does the need for additional faculty arise. In today's institutions, some have focused on utilizing adjunct, contingent, or part-time faculty as a way to control expenses while still provide qualified instruction. There are benefits to this model—adjuncts, contingent, and part-time faculty do not require the additional expenses of employment benefits, space on campus, or long-term commitments. If a program begins to falter, contracts with part-time faculty can be nonrenewable and no long-term expectation for employment is built.

As a new academic program developer, you will likely face questions regarding how many faculty will be needed to start the program, in what capacity, and when faculty might need to be added (or reduced) in the future. How many faculty does a new academic program truly need? And what is the formula for determining that a new program has enough faculty to offer quality education without overspending on faculty salaries and benefits? There are several considerations when hiring or assigning faculty to a new academic program. These include:

- Student-to-faculty ratio (how many faculty are needed may be directly tied to how many students the program is capable of enrolling)
- Intensity of coursework or program requirements. Activities like internships, dissertations, laboratory experiences, or fieldwork can increase the need for faculty oversight (and time).
- Available faculty are already employed at the institution. This can be both a positive and a negative situation when an institution seeks to realign existing faculty to new program responsibilities. We've witnessed situations where faculty are moved between departments without conversation about interest or expertise, where faculty are assigned "overload" courses without compensation, or where faculty are asked to work within a new program temporarily until more faculty can be hired. While utilizing existing faculty can be a wise financial decision, it is also asking faculty with disciplinary expertise to be open to a different type of academic process—one that not every typical tenure-track or teaching/research faculty will be interested in or want to take time away from their own scholarly pursuits to serve.
- Part of estimating faculty needs is considering how many and what resources will be allocated to help the faculty member(s) build the new

program. Administrative support, staff roles, financial planning expertise, and time to complete administrative tasks can become overwhelming. Many institutions ignore the demand this places on the faculty developer's time and energy—and clearly, it should be accounted for upfront.

There is no clear formula to accurately predict the number of faculty needed to establish a new academic program. Depending on individual work styles, strengths, and administrative capacity, some programs can survive with one or two faculty members for a while, whereas other programs show a clear need for many more dedicated faculty. The analysis in this area should be a purposeful exploration of where time needs to be spent, who has the talents to contribute to the program, and where obvious weaknesses are present. Then, and only then, should an estimate of the number, FTE, and assignment of faculty be considered.

NAVIGATING YOUR OWN FACULTY ROLE

Whether you are a tenure-track, tenured, or part-time faculty member, moving into new academic proposal and design is a shift from what might be considered the traditional duties of faculty. Think about how most college and university faculty functioned only a few decades ago: most held terminal degrees in an academic discipline; the primary role of faculty was to teach courses in face-to-face settings, and the remainder of their time was dedicated to research and publication or service to the institution.

Our experiences as faculty tasked with new academic program development and implementation lead us to explore how this type of process does not fit neatly into the typical "teaching/research/service" buckets that define most faculty contracts. In fact, time spent curating a strong proposal, building connections with campus stakeholders, and outlining budget and marketing plans is often not considered scholarly activity in some institutions. While it clearly is something that will likely benefit the institution, it shifts traditional faculty roles into those more like an entrepreneur—where time is spent in new and varied activities, building new processes, and learning the layers of institutional administration.

We raise this point so that you can think about your own role—whether it be a tenure-track line within a department or as a part-time instructor, your work will change as you engage in these processes. And likely, no one will be protecting your best interests to ensure that your tenure requirements are met or that your teaching evaluations remain strong. You will need to be your own advocate in that regard. Specifically, there are several areas for faculty to consider about their faculty role when moving into new program development:

1. How will the new academic program development impact your teaching or research load? Will you be designing new curricula and teaching for it? Will this be in addition to or in lieu of your other teaching or research responsibilities?
2. Is there an expected credit hour production that you are responsible for regardless of your role as a new academic program developer? If so, how can that be met?
3. How will your faculty time load be measured within the traditional "buckets" of research, service, and teaching? Where do the activities involved with new academic program development fit, and will your administration support your work as an untraditional way to meet the typical requirements within those areas?
4. How can you sustain a research path when much of your time is consumed with new academic program development?

Again, you are the best advocate for yourself in this process. Be clear as you accept new responsibilities, duties, and time-intensive activities that what was your prior job may be shifting—maybe even unintentionally.

ADVOCATING FOR MORE PERSONNEL OVER TIME

The hope of every new academic program development is that it will draw so many students that there is no choice but to grow the program—and this will mean adding faculty and staff. What typically starts as a one- or two-person team is faced with the challenge of finding, hiring, and, most likely, supervising additional faculty and staff, whether they are new to the institution or not. While initial budget projections are future-oriented, the addition of new employees at most institutions is not an easy process. Some institutions require multiple layers of approval in order to create a new position, whereas others refuse to hire any full-time roles until a program shows long-term, stable growth.

When is the right time to begin advocating for more faculty or staff? It depends. There are a few telltale signs that a new program is growing at such a rate (or simply requires more resources in order to function properly):

- Are you and the other new academic program developer(s) multitasking at an unsustainable pace? We've seen this when faculty leading new programs serve as the program director, student advisor, curriculum committee chair, admissions committee chair, and course instructor for several courses simultaneously.
- Is the student experience jeopardized because of the lack of time or attention to detail provided by the program personnel?

- Are deadlines regularly missed for routine institutional paperwork or duties?
- Is the student-to-faculty ratio higher than recommended by the accrediting agency or professional organizations within the discipline?
- Are working conditions within the new academic program team faltering due to burnout, job stress, or poor time management?

In short, we suggest keeping a best-case scenario mindset. That is, if the new program grows and meets or exceeds enrollment projections, demand support for additional personnel to ensure the program CAN grow and grow in a meaningful way. This does not always align well with institutional financial planners or budget keepers, but in any industry, to grow, resources need to be devoted to that growth. Growing a new academic program should be no different.

PART-TIME AND FULL-TIME ADDITIONS TO THE TEAM

Faculty within new academic programs can serve in many forms—from full-time, tenure-track faculty to part-time adjunct or contingent roles. As you build a new academic program, consider what team of faculty, staff, and others would be ideal. And how can new members be identified, hired, and onboarded in a meaningful way? It's not uncommon in new programs today that the number of part-time, non-tenure-track faculty outnumbers the amount of full-time faculty also working within the program. What nuances of the program do contingent faculty teaching a class or two need to know or understand?

Careful consideration needs to be paid to who is doing what and in what capacity. In simpler terms, part-time faculty are limited in the scope of their responsibilities and commitment to an institution. In 1980, the AAUP noted several limitations to working as a part-time faculty member, including the lack of participation in faculty governance, lack of employment security, the absence of fringe benefits like health insurance or retirement contributions, and a disconnect with the university community. Thus, while part-time or contingent faculty might be the easiest to find and cheapest to hire, do these conditions create the academic environment necessary to best shepherds growth and retention of students?

Additionally, as we've pointed out in other chapters and sections in this book, as a faculty member, you probably have little to no training in the institutional hiring processes. Aside from when you completed your own onboarding paperwork, your conversations with the Human Resources office at your institution may be few and far between. As a program leader, you will need to begin to understand how and when new personnel can and should be added. There may be institutional formulas that need to be calculated in terms of student-to-faculty ratio or growth potential percentages. You will probably also need to learn how to navigate your institution's HR website where job announcements are listed and applications are sorted. Lastly, you may need to explore and determine if there are required protocols for campus visits, interview meetings, or reference checks on potential candidates. While you will be supported by an HR professional, most likely, the onus of working through these processes to hire the best fit of people for the new academic program will be on your shoulders.

GROWING OTHERS AND YOURSELF AT THE SAME TIME

Once you've hired new faculty, it is important to consider their professional requirements and growth needs. For tenure-track faculty, this may mean building processes to annually review teaching evaluations, publication rates, and service to the institution. For tenured faculty, this could involve identifying ways to help seasoned academics identify and progress toward professional growth goals. For staff, this might involve completing annual performance assessments, seeking input from others on the performance of duties, or even releasing staff from duties.

As a new program developer, you are tasked with looking beyond your own needs. You may still be in professional growth mode, so mentoring someone else may be a bit unsettling. While there are many resources on how to be a strong academic mentor, some commonalities within the advice about this area include learning to ask open-ended questions, taking time to build a meaningful, personal relationship with the mentee, seeking out professional development workshops or opportunities, and providing networking opportunities to build on relationships you may already have and can extend to the new hire. One resource you might share with new faculty might be Marybeth Gasman's book titled *Candid Advice for New Faculty Members: A Guide to Getting Tenure and Advancing Your Academic Career,* an accessible and straightforward book designed for new faculty seeking career advancement in academia.

SHARING FACULTY

New academic programs often bring up that old saying about building processes as they are happening, as "building the plane while flying." No one wants to be the first passenger on a plane that isn't fully constructed, yet this is often how faculty are tapped to join a new program. Some new academic programs must utilize existing faculty to teach courses or serve as project supervisors. This can be a positive experience wherein the silos of academic disciplines can be crossed and an interdisciplinary lens is created. This can also be the exact opposite—a situation where faculty are asked to spend time outside of their established discipline to help a start-up program offer courses with less than ideal enrollment or an unknown future.

Politically, sharing faculty with other departments, disciplines, colleges, or units can feel like a field of landmines that need to be carefully treaded. Some contentious issues we've seen arise in programs where faculty are shared across programs include

A lack of clarity about how much time the faculty member spends when spread over multiple programs or departments

Confusion over who supervises and evaluates these faculty

Distrust or discontent when a faculty member does not want to join a new program, teach new courses, or work with students in a different capacity

Friction between program deans or chairs with assumptions that one is trying to steal faculty

Tenuous relationships between faculty, staff, and others due to the stress of new program growth and management

Sharing faculty across departments, disciplines, or colleges can make sound financial sense on paper, but political challenges are inherent as no sharing relationship is without conflict or confusion. Transparent, well-documented, and frequent conversations with both the shared faculty and administrators of the entities sharing are essential.

Sharing the To-Do List with Faculty

Within any new academic program, there will be an emerging and constantly changing "to-do" list. When faculty ranks expand, so, too, does the necessity to align faculty with tasks, assignments, and other responsibilities that help strengthen a program. Go back and review the Universal Framework for a New Academic Proposal we shared in chapter 2. At the time of development, you were projecting and imagining a future that was unknown. Once students are settled into their classes and processes are beginning to flow, it's time to delegate to your faculty partners.

Not all tasks within new program development can be delegated. Some things need to remain on your list as the program developer—like working with the marketing team on building the right language to draw students to the program or working with the finance team to ensure incoming tuition is attributed to the right places. Other processes, like establishing curriculum and assessment committees, reviewing student admissions applications, updating course policies, or articulating advising practices, can and should be delegated. We argue this not because these tasks are simple, but rather delegating these types of responsibilities will allow you to spend your time on the larger roles of program development, like finding new avenues of student audiences to reach, building partnerships with community organizations, and finding external funding opportunities.

In short, as you begin working with other faculty, build on their strengths so that you can keep using yours to strengthen the new academic program. Find avenues to share responsibilities that were once yours but can be trusted to others. Build strong processes for delegation wherein you do more than simply unload a task on a colleague, but engage in a meaningful dialogue about what needs to be done and develop opportunities where feedback and questions can be addressed. This not only expands the capacity of program personnel but also shifts some of your responsibilities into supervisory rather than active—and by the time the program is at this stage, you will need this respite. Recruiting, hiring, and retaining faculty for a new academic program is an exciting prospect—it means finding others, like you, who share an excitement for new projects. It also demands that you, someone who once probably occupied your own faculty position, learn how to find, mentor, and shepherd other professionals as they gain more experience. Because your new program proposal was strong in its initial inception, faculty considerations during the implementation phases of a new program are wide and varied, from considering how you will fulfill your own institutional responsibilities to how you will tame the temper of a dean who is unhappy about sharing faculty across colleges.

QUESTIONS FOR YOUR REFLECTION

1. What is the unique role of each faculty member added to the new program? How do positions differ, and how are they similar?
2. Where can professional growth opportunities emerge that can help all faculty in the new program expand their scholarly knowledge?
3. Where can you gain support in assisting others in their tenure or promotion processes?
4. How will you identify tasks that can be delegated to other faculty members?
5. Where are your blind spots for faculty recruitment, hiring, and development? Where can you go to learn more about these areas specifically?
6. What sort of support do you need from your department or college's leadership to successfully hire new faculty members?

7. Where did you need support most when you entered higher education? How can you fill those gaps today?
8. What challenges lie ahead for someone new to academia within your academic program? How can you articulate these to the new faculty?
9. What skill sets will best balance those you already have in your new program?

Chapter 8

Reflections about Leading, Building, and Implementation

Overview: Conceptualizing, designing, proposing, building, and implementing a new academic program can be an invigorating experience for anyone in academia. It can also be fraught with challenges, missteps, and complete disasters. In this last chapter, we share some insights we've had within our own work as new academic program leaders, advice we'd share with a new academic program leader today, and things we wish we would have known a lot earlier in the process.

THE THRILL OF LEADING

In many ways, we capture our experiences of proposing, building, and leading new academic proposals to be much like ABC sports broadcaster Jim McKay's opening line to the old TV show *Wide World of Sports,* where opened each week's show with the same phrase: "the thrill of victory and the agony of defeat" (Miller, 2008, para. 7). There are many parts of leading a new academic program that are challenging and invigorating all at once. You are creating something new, allowed to be innovative, untethered by the past, and can create new ways of learning that will lead your institution into the future.

You are trusted and tasked with a great deal of responsibility, from building a program with fidelity and accurate information to carrying out the mission and vision of the institution. Whether you are given a formal leadership title or not, you are a decision-maker in thinking about how to design a new program, the types of students that might be attracted to the program, and how that learning can change the landscape for today's graduates.

There's a great deal of freedom that can come with new academic program leadership. Often, you are left to design components alone, without much help, which means you get to choose the best of your ideas. Even if working with a team, your expertise is often deferred to as the best in the room. Additionally, you build your CV with experiences different from those of any traditional faculty role. You are no longer only teaching or researching, but you are creating, designing, and building something brand new. Your vision of your own career begins to shift and evolve.

Accompanying these benefits is also the potential for continuous growth. You can learn about yourself as a leader, understand how to lead in higher education, and begin to understand processes you may have never even known existed. You can develop courses that are unique, challenging, and creative, and you can work with students in manners untethered by traditional learning methods. You might be considered for other positions on campus or find that leadership is something you want to pursue.

As a new academic program leader, you will also have the possibility to build relationships that would have never formed had you stayed in your traditional faculty role. Not only will you be working with new students (or students new to you), but you will be making connections with people in other areas that make the institution run—from accounting to finance to higher-level leadership, to connections at other institutions. You will learn from these interactions, and without having a new program to advocate for, you may not have even entered the room in the first place.

THE AGONY OF LEADING

While leading a new academic program can indeed be thrilling, it can also create a sense of agony—about your career, your place in the institution, your intelligence, and your decision-making ability. Leadership is hard, and just because you are leading something new and exciting does not mean everyone will support your work. You may run into colleagues who are consistently undermining or questioning your work, or you may find that what was once promised by the institution is later reduced or rescinded.

Interactions with people in leadership can be fraught with challenges. Leaders often have competing interests, so you will find yourself "selling" your program time and again to keep the idea fresh, relevant, and to ensure continued buy-in. You may be hesitant to share when things do not go well and may hide some of the challenges you face. Additionally, you may find other leaders with more established patterns or relationships have an easier time accomplishing things than you.

Leadership is also very lonely. Even if you work with a team, when you lead a new academic program, you are generally "the" signature that approves new processes, that hires new faculty and staff, and that admits or dismisses students. In that, you may have few trusted colleagues to confer with, and you may wonder if the course of action you take is the most appropriate. You will seek approval from others—campus leaders, potential students, other staff on campus—and few may recognize the amount of work you are putting into your efforts. Additionally, you may be doing all of this on top of your original job—which means time away from home or your personal pursuits becomes very limited—and again, lonely.

Failure is inherent in leadership—and while we've promoted that as a good thing within program development, it is also something that most humans dread and fear. We often work to avoid failure at all costs. However, in this type of work—where creating and building are essential to implementation—failure will happen. It will not feel good. It may make you question your worth, your abilities, or your drive to complete what you've started. It can be entirely agonizing.

ADVICE TO A NEW ACADEMIC PROGRAM LEADER

As we've conferred through our crafting of this book, we started a series of Post-It Notes with advice we'd give new academic program leaders. We ended up with seven of these, and they included the following advice (from lived experiences):

1. Use the chance to propose, build, and implement a new program as a way to do something different. Don't feel confined by the way other programs run at your institution. Very few faculty get the chance to invent, so learn how to be an inventor.
2. Be prepared to learn everything about your institution. We've covered this in several different places throughout this book, but we cannot overemphasize how important it will be to learn the actual structures of the institution—the things that make it run like a business, such as finance, HR, and planning. The more you know and understand about the processes that even minorly touch your program, the better you can lead.
3. Feign confidence: We embrace the "fake it until you make it" approach to new program leadership. Granted, you should not misrepresent your abilities, but sometimes a sense of confidence will be convincing when others are challenging your decision-making processes or wondering if your work will prove to be successful.

4. Learn the boring stuff. Before leading new academic programs, neither of us had ever seen a department or college budget form. We had never filled out a budget planning document nor had we considered the true cost of hiring a faculty member (there's salary plus benefits and other expenses the institution will incur). It will never be as exciting as the area you spent years earning your PhD, but it is necessary nonetheless. Doing so will not only help you streamline and understand processes, but will also build your confidence in your decision-making.
5. Make decisions with finality: One aspect of leading a new academic program that has shown up time and time again in our lives has been the need to make swift and firm decisions. This might mean rejecting impossible timelines for completion, finalizing instructional choices, or pushing back against an institution that wants you to enroll more students than are feasible within the size of the program you have.
6. Write your own story: Through the process of conceptualizing, proposing, and building a new academic program, you will hear advice from all types of people—colleagues, friends, people outside of the institution, people from other institutions, and even your own leaders. While it can be tempting to replicate the work of others, what matters most is that your program stands out in the wide landscape of programs available to students today. This means that you are an integral piece of the program design—your talent, expertise, and knowledge bring an angle that no one else has, so build on that.
7. Don't forget who you are: Assuming a role within a new academic program can be thrilling and challenging, but it can also change your perceptions about your institution, higher education, and your discipline. Even though you are tasked with leadership decisions, remember your academic training—the drive for thorough examination, understanding problems, and scholarly pursuits.

THINGS WE KNOW NOW THAT WE WISH WE WOULD'VE LEARNED EARLIER

In addition to the advice we'd give to a new academic program leader today, we also generated some things we wish we had known back in the days when we were building and launching our respective new academic programs. These included:

1. Leadership is hard (really, hard). Yes, it can be great and fulfilling and wonderful, but it can also be difficult, controversial, and the kind of thing that keeps you up all night thinking about the problems you are

facing. While leadership can be lonely and highly independent, it can also be isolating and depressing. Becoming a leader without any formal leadership training has its own challenges from the start, including not recognizing known areas of conflict or predicting things that may steadily fall apart. Had we known how difficult leadership would be, we would have prepared ourselves with a wider network of individuals that we could turn to in times of crisis or disappointment. That network, it seems, is what makes leadership bearable.
2. Some people are not ready for change. Even when an institution fully embraces launching a new academic program, there will be people within, some even close colleagues, who will question your work and undermine your efforts. Some will say the new program is a waste of time or will decrease the academic rigor or prestige of the institution. Others will see it as a "pet project" of campus leadership or an attempt to capture the newest ideas in the marketplace that will quickly lose their appeal. It's best to understand that not everyone will have the same drive, passion, or persistence to build a new program—and that's ok. You can do it without them and in spite of them.
3. Get what you can in writing. Through both of our new program-building processes, we both experienced times when what was said and what was done in actuality were two different things. For example, one campus leader might promise a commitment of funds only to have that commitment overturned by the college dean. Others will boast that they have a known connection to a full cohort of students ready to enroll in your program, yet are unable to produce the connection. The more you can get in writing, as tedious as it can be, can help you when things go backward or promises go unmet. Granted, no one likes to be confronted with an email they sent or information they may have shared erroneously, but your goal should be to have clarity in all decisions, and having agreements, aspirations, commitments, and input in writing can be very beneficial.
4. Anticipate guessing. A lot. Even with the best new academic program proposals, there is a lot of guessing involved. You'll make educated guesses about what students are willing to pay for tuition rates, how many students you'll have in the upcoming terms, or how many graduates will be employed in the field. You'll oftentimes guess on tapping a certain market with advertisements only to have it yield no interest. You'll also hold promotional events or enrollment fairs where you meet several interested students who do not end up in actual enrollment. You'll guess about the right number of students within a course, the actual need for faculty before you have ongoing enrollment patterns, and the amount of money you'll need on an annual basis. This is not

nefarious guessing, but simply the nature of how the process goes. Even the best marketing campaigns can yield no students or ten times the number of students you anticipated—so until you have time to experience the program in action, guessing will be much of what you do.
5. No one will love your program like you do. Not to sound too emotional here, but there is a certain level of affection that a new academic program leader holds for a program that they build from the ground up. Not only does it involve a lot of time and work, but it also requires an investment in the belief that the program will do well, will change the landscape of education, and will reach students in new and unique ways. That being said, no matter how supportive your campus leaders are, they will likely never have this same appreciation for how long it took to build or how decisive you had to be to get a program into fruition. They may never understand the nuances you discovered when building this program in a slightly different way from other programs or the different learning opportunities that students in this program will have.

CONCLUSION

We both agree that the time we've spent in our careers proposing, building, implementing, and advocating for the new academic programs we've represented has been exceptionally worthwhile. The work was challenging, frustrating, and invigorating all at the same time. It allowed us to stretch our leadership skills into areas we had not explored before, and it provided opportunities for us to meet people we would have never met had we stayed within the confines of our classrooms. It pushed each of us not only to become more passionate about our disciplines but also to better understand the larger structures within which we work. We both will openly share that we did not go into higher education with aspirations to lead or to start a new academic program, yet here we are, reflecting on the good and bad of those events.

As you can now see, there is no defined road to building and leading a new academic program. What we did in our journeys will differ from the steps that you may be required to take or the hurdles or support that you earn along the way. Know that the work is important. Higher education is changing, and we cannot remain stagnant with our feet stuck in our disciplinary practices. The more open we are to innovation, creating new learning opportunities, and discovering how students can use the content they learn in our courses within their own professional fields, the more excited we can be about the future that lies ahead in our careers.

References

AACSB (2024). *AACSB accreditation.* AACSB. https://www.aacsb.edu/educators/accreditation

Adame, J. (2023, March 20). Field of study not key to new academic program success. *Inside Higher Ed.* https://www.insidehighered.com/news/2023/03/21/field-study-not-key-new-academic-program-success#

American Association of University Professors (1980). *The status of part-time faculty.* AAUP.org. https://www.aaup.org/report/status-part-time-faculty

American Immigration Council (2023, Aug. 2). Undocumented college students: How many students are in U.S. colleges and universities, and who are they? *American Immigration Council.* https://www.americanimmigrationcouncil.org/research/undocumented-college-students-2023

American Psychological Association (2024). Trends for 2024. *American Psychological Association.* https://www.apa.org/monitor/2024/01/trends-higher-education-challenges

Armstrong, P. (2010). Bloom's Taxonomy. *Vanderbilt University Center for Teaching.* https://cft.vanderbilt.edu/guides-sub-pages/blooms-taxonomy/

Auburn University (2024). Our vision. *Auburn University.* https://auburn.edu/about/visionandmission.php

Boston University (n.d.) Creating learning outcomes. *Boston University Provost.* https://www.bu.edu/provost/files/2017/06/Creating-Learning-Outcomes-Stanford.pdf

Burning Glass Technologies (2020). Bad bets: The high cost of failing programs in higher education. *Lightcast.io.* https://4906807.fs1.hubspotusercontent-na1.net/hubfs/4906807/BGT-reports/BGT_BADBETS.pdf

Carnegie Higher Ed (2018, May 16). Ready for launch: A guide eto positioning your new academic program for success. *Carnegie.* https://www.carnegiehighered.com/blog/ready-for-launch-a-guide-to-positioning-your-new-academic-program-for-success/

Center for First Generation Student Success (2020). National data fact sheets on first generation college students and graduates. *NASPA.* https://firstgen.naspa.org/

journal-and-research/national-data-fact-sheets-on-first-generation-college-students-and-graduates

Chronicle Intelligence (2024). Who is a first-generation student. *The Chronicle of Higher Education*. https://www.chronicle.com/featured/student-success/student-centric-institution/who-is-a-first-generation-student

Cote, C. (2020, Oct. 6). Why is strategic planning important? *Harvard Business School Online*. https://online.hbs.edu/blog/post/why-is-strategic-planning-important

Drucker, P. F. (2009). *The essential Drucker: The best of sixty years of Peter Drucker's essential writings on management.* Harper Collins.

Dweck, C. S. (2019). The choice to make a difference. *Perspectives on Psychological Science, 14*(1), 21–25. https://doi.org/10.1177/1745691618804180

Elliott, K. (2023, Feb. 24). Why mentorship is even more important when you're a leader. *Forbes.com*. https://www.forbes.com/sites/forbescoachescouncil/2023/02/24/why-mentorship-is-even-more-important-when-youre-a-leader/

Farson, R. & Keyes, R. (2022, Aug). The failure-tolerant leader. *Harvard Business Review*. Harvard Business Publishing.

Glendale Community College (2022). Institutional learning outcomes (ILOs). *Glendale Community College*. https://www.glendale.edu/about-gcc/faculty-and-staff/learning-outcomes/institutional-learning-outcomes

Grand View Research (2024). Higher education market size, share & trends report, 2030. *Grand View Research*. https://www.grandviewresearch.com/industry-analysis/higher-education-market

Hanson, M. (2024, Jan. 10). College enrollment and student demographic statistics. *Education Data Initiative*. https://educationdata.org/college-enrollment-statistics

Harvard Business School. Our mission. *Harvard Business School*. https://www.hbs.edu/about/mission

Harvard College (2024). Mission, vision, and history. *Harvard.edu*. https://college.harvard.edu/about/mission-vision-history

Higher Ed Immigration Portal (2024). *National data*. https://www.higheredimmigrationportal.org/national/national-data/

Higher Ed Immigration Portal (2024). *States*. https://www.higheredimmigrationportal.org/states/

Howath, R. (2005). Discovering purpose: Developing mission, vision & values. *Strategic Thinking Institute*. https://www.strategyskills.com/Articles/Documents/Discovering_Purpose-STI.pdf

Knowles, M. (1990). *The adult learner: A neglected species.* Gulf Publishing Company.

Koenig, R. (2019, Nov. 25). 'Academic capitalism' is reshaping faculty life. What does that mean? *EdSurge*. https://www.edsurge.com/news/2019-11-25-academic-capitalism-is-reshaping-faculty-life-what-does-that-mean

Lane, I. F. (2007). Change in higher education: Unverstanding and responding to individual and organizational resistance. *Journal of Veterinary Medical Education, 34(2)*, 85–92.

Marcus, J. (2019, Jan. 19). 10 years later, goal of getting more Americans through college is way behind schedule. *Hechinger Report*. https://hechingerreport.org/10-years-later-goal-of-getting-more-americans-through-college-is-way-behind-schedule/

Marcus, J. (2021, Oct. 3). From Google ads to NFL sponsorships: Colleges throw billions at marketing themselves to attract students. *Washington Post*. https://www.washingtonpost.com/local/education/colleges-marketing-student-recruitment/2021/09/30/b6ddd246-2166-11ec-8200-5e3fd4c49f5e_story.html

Miller, D. (2008, June 14). Jim McKay: The thrill of victory…the agony of defeat. *Bleacher Report*. https://bleacherreport.com/articles/29612-jim-mckay-the-thrill-of-victorythe-agony-of-defeat

National Leadership Council for Liberal Education, America's Promise. (2007). *College learning for the new global century*. Association of American Colleges and Universities.

Northouse, P. G. (2021). *Introduction to leadership: Concepts and practices*. SAGE Publications.

North Carolina State University (2024). University mission. https://leadership.ncsu.edu/university-mission/

Nuoman, A. (2022, Sept. 29). Success and failure rates of new academic programs. *Elliance*. https://aha.elliance.com/2022/09/29/success-and-failure-rates-of-new-academic-programs/

Santa Clara University (2024). The assessment process. *Santa Clara University*. https://www.scu.edu/provost/institutional-effectiveness/assessment/the-assessment-process/

Schermele, Z. (2024, Jan. 24). College enrollments are rebounding after the pandemic. *USA Today*. https://www.usatoday.com/story/news/education/2024/01/24/college-enrollments-growing-after-pandemic/72341166007/

Schoolkraft, T. (2016, Nov. 18). Overcoming barriers to new program development. *evolllution.com*. https://evolllution.com/programming/program_planning/overcoming-barriers-to-new-program-development

St. Bonaventure University (2012). Governing documents. *St. Bonaventure University*. https://web.sbu.edu/friedsam/governing/academic_policies/academic_programs_new.htm

University of Minnesota (2024). *University student learning and development outcomes*. University of Minnesota. https://slo.umn.edu/undergraduate-experience/university-student-learning-development-outcomes

Univeristy of Missouri (2024). How to write program outcomes. *University of Missouri Provost*. https://provost.missouri.edu/programs-centers/program-assessments/assessment-of-student-learning/how-to-write-program-outcomes/

United States Department of Veterans Affairs (n.d). *VA campus toolkit handout*. https://www.mentalhealth.va.gov/student-veteran/docs/VAM-061-VITAL-Characteristics-of-Student-Veterans-1-0-508.pdf

Vyletel, B., Voichoski, E., Lipson, S. & Heinze, J. (2023, Aug. 31). Exploring faculty burnout through the 2022-23 HMS faculty/staff survey. *American Psychological*

Association. https://www.apa.org/ed/precollege/psychology-teacher-network/introductory-psychology/faculty-burnout-survey

Welding, L. (2023, April 6). Women in higher education: 5 key facts and statistics. *Best Colleges.* https://www.bestcolleges.com/research/women-in-higher-education-facts-statistics/

Index

academic capitalist regime, 44
accreditation, 13, 66–67
adapting to the unknown, 73
adaption setting of leading, 76–77
administrative/program leadership, 73
adult learners, 81
advocating for more personnel over time, 93–94
agony of leading, 100–101
alignment with institutional outcomes, 60–61
American Association of Colleges and Schools of Business (AACSB), 30
American Association of Colleges and Universities (AAC&U), 86
Americans with Disabilities Act, 83
Andragogy, 81
Anticipated Support Channels, 34
A Perfect Mess (Labaree), 6
asking meaningful questions, 74
assessment, 65–66
Auburn University, 46
authoritarian, 75

bad bet, 55
barriers to new program development, 48–49
belonging, 87

benefits: to the faculty, 6–7; to the institution, 5–6; to the student, 7–8
Bloom's Taxonomy, 64–65
Boston University, 61–62
budgets, 55, 76–77; demands, 13
building. *See* reflections
building and launching, new academic programs: anticipate guessing, 103–4; leadership, 102–3; love your program, 104; not ready for change, 103; writing, 103
building on existing foundations, 46; mission, 47; strategic plan, 47–48; vision, 46–47
building our respective programs, 71–72

Candid Advice for New Faculty Members: A Guide to Getting Tenure and Advancing Your Academic Career (Gasman), 95
capital costs, 34
The Carnegie Higher Education, 23
challenges, 72; of self-doubt, 15
collaboration, essential development skill, 56–57
communication, 61; clarity, 54; frequently, 54
components of, typical proposal, 21; accreditation considerations, 30;

assessment processes, 29; faculty hiring, 28–29; future/predicting a program budget, 26–27; mode of delivery, 24; need for the program, 22; policy development, 28; potential student market, 22–23; program outcomes, 23; rationale, 21–22; required coursework, 26; resources, 29; student applications, 24–25; student enrollment, 25–26; timeline of implementation, 26
comprehensive proposal elements, 30; section 1: program description, 31; section 2: rationale for the program, 32; section 3: evidence of need for the program, 33; section 4: cost of a new program, 34–35; section 5: similar and related programs, 36; section 6: preparation for ongoing education, 37; section 7: quality and other aspects of the program, 38–40; section 8: students, projected headcount, and FTE enrollments and degrees conferred, 41
Conroy, Edward, 84
considerations: hiring/assigning faculty, 91–92; new academic program leaders, 81–85
costs, 34; of hiring/retaining, faculty member, 28–29; and support for program, 34–35
Cote, Catherine, 47
Council on Education for Public Health (CEPH), 66
coursework, 83
crafting course learning outcomes, 63–64
creating program outcomes, 61–63
critical thinking, 61

Deferred Action for Childhood Arrivals (DACA), 84–85
democratic, 75
doctoral programs, 28
Drucker, Peter, 46
Dweck, Carol, 72

education, 5–6
The Education Data Initiative, 85
embrace change, 54
embracing a growth mindset, 72–73
English department, 49
enrollment management, 24
ensuring outcomes encourage learning, 64–65
estimating faculty needs, new academic program, 91–92
evidence of need for the program, 33
external considerations, 13

faculty, 34, 66; assignment, 91; considerations, 89; developer, 53–54; guiding question for, 8–9; involvement, 13–14; role in program development, 92–93; and staff, 34
failure, 101; within leadership, 76–77
Farson, R., 76
feign confidence, 101
finality decision, 102
first-generation students, 82
formula for program outcome design, 63
FTE enrollment and degrees, 41

Gasman, Marybeth, 95
global higher education market size, 45
Goldstein, Larry, 26–27
growing, 92–93, 95

Harvard Business School, 47
Harvard College, 46–47
Hechinger Report, 4
hidden curriculum, 82
high cost of innovation, 55
higher education, 56, 76–77, 80. *See also individual entries*
high-impact practices, 86
Human Resources, 94–95

immigrant students, 84–85
implementation. *See* reflections
importance of faculty, 89–90
information to lead a new academic program, 86–87

in-person classroom learning (traditional), 24
institution, 9, 12, 101
institutional culture, 55
institutional leaders, 49
intensity of coursework or program requirements, 91
internal considerations, 13
internal *vs.* external barriers, 48–49
international students, 83–84
The IPEDS System (Integrated Postsecondary Education Data System), 85

K-12 teacher education program, 64–65
Keyes, R., 76
knowledge, skills, abilities and attitudes, 60–61
Knowles, Malcolm, 81

Labaree, David, 6
lack of training, 72
Laissez-faire, 75
Lane, India, 53–54
launch of: challenge of self-doubt, 15; development and implementation, 5; faculty benefit, 6–7; guiding question for faculty, 8–9; institution benefit, 5–6; leading and learning adventure, 14–15; overview, 3–4; processes, strategies, and people necessity, 11–14; purpose of reflection and guiding process, 17; status of educational institutions, 4; student benefit, 7–8; understanding the place of program, 9–11; use of, 15–17
layers, 49–50
leadership, 100–101; styles of, 75
leadership 101, 72; adapting, 73; collaborate, 73; embracing growth mindset, 72–73; promoting student achievement and faculty growth, 74; questions, 74
leadership mentors, 75–76

leading: efforts to, 75; leadership style, 74–75; and learning adventure, 14–15; types of leadership, 74. *See also* reflections
leading students, new academic program, 79–80; high-impact practices, 86; overview, 79–80; student demographics data, 85–86; types of students, 80–85; use of information, 86–87
lean leadership, 1; failure within leadership, 76–77; innovation, flexibility, adeptness, 71–72; leadership 101, new academic program leaders, 72–74; leadership mentors, 75–76; prioritizing self-care, 77–78; working on, 74–75
learning, 102
learning outcomes: active verbs in future tense, 62; alignment, 60; align with program's curriculum, 62; framed in terms of program, 62; products focus and not process, 63; realistic, 62; simple and not compound, 62; specific and well defined, 61–62; sufficient number of, 62

market-driven culture of academia, 45–46
McClure, Kevin, 44
McKay, Jim, 99
mentors, 76
military veterans, 82
mission, 13, 47

national, state, or regional need, 33
National Student Clearinghouse® Research Center™, 80
nature of support, 34
navigating your own faculty role, 92–93
new academic program, 48. *See also individual entries*
new academic program leaders, 72, 100; adaptation, 73; advice to, 101–2; asking meaningful questions, 74;

embracing growth mindset, 72–73; promoting student achievement and faculty growth, 74
new academic proposals, 19–20, 90; components of, 21–30; comprehensive elements, 30–41; planning necessity, 20; universal framework, 20–21
new program, 9; approvals, 49–50; design and development, 43–44
new undergraduate and graduate degree programs, 55
North Carolina State University's mission, 47
Northouse, P. G., 75

online learning (virtual), 24
organizational culture, 55–56
organizing for student learning, 59; accreditation, 66–67; alignment with institutional outcomes, 60–61; assessment, 65–66; Bloom's Taxonomy, 65; crafting course learning outcomes, 63–64; creating program outcomes, 61–63; ensuring outcomes encourage learning, 64–65; formula for program outcome design, 63; learning outcomes alignment, 60; prioritizing learning in new program development, 59–60; typical learning outcomes alignment, 60
"Overcoming Barriers to New Program Development" (Schoolkraft), 48–49

part of estimating faculty needs, 91–92
part-time and full-time additions to the team, 94–95
part-time faculty, 94
part-time students, 83
perceptions, 102
political maneuverings and persuasive language: academic capitalist regime, 44; collaboration, development skill, 56–57; high cost of innovation, 55; internal *vs.* external barriers, 48–49; layers, 49–50; market-driven culture of academia, 45–46; mission, vision, and strategic planning, 46–48; organizational culture, 55–56; overview, 43–44; proposing, designing and implementing, 48; resistance to change, 53–54; role of stakeholders, 51–53
post-pandemic higher education environment, 79
preparation for ongoing education , 37
preparing to lead faculty, 89; advocating for more personnel over time, 93–94; estimating faculty needs, new academic program, 91–92; growing others and yourself at the same time, 95; the importance of faculty, 89–90; navigating your own faculty role, 92–93; part-time and full-time additions to the team, 94–95; sharing faculty, 95–97
prioritizing learning in new program development, 59–60
prioritizing self-care, 77–78
problem-solving, 61
professional growth, 77, 95
program: accreditation, 38; architect, 21; aspects of, 38–40; assessment, 38; courses, 38; credit hours, 38; description, 31; developer, 54; directors, 71–72; job titles, 40; learning outcomes, 39; placement of graduates, 38–39; quality, 38–39; student engagement experiences with career relevance, 39. *See also individual entries*
promoting student achievement and faculty growth, 74
propose, build, and implement a new program, 101
purpose of reflection and guiding process, 17

rationale for the program (need and justification), 32

recognize your weaknesses and seek advice, 54
recommended leadership traits, 74
reflections, 99; advice to new academic program leader, 101–2; agony of leading, 100–101; building and launching, respective new academic programs, 102–4; synopsis, 104; thrill of leading, 99–100
resistance to change, 53–54
role of stakeholders, 51; goals and outcomes alignment, 52; interest, 51–52; long-term relationship, benefit students and faculty, 53; seeking to gain, 52–53; working closely, help/harm, 52

sample budget template, 35
Santa Clara University, 65–66
Schoolkraft, Tracy, 48–49
sex and gender, 80–81
sharing faculty, 95–97
sharing the to-do list with faculty, 96–97
shifting academic teaching/research faculty, 72
similar and related programs, 36
specialized knowledge, 61
speech communications course, 63
Stakeholders in the new academic proposal process, 51
standing in the middle of chaos: accreditation questions, 13; acknowledge, 11–12; budget demands, 13; external considerations, 13; faculty/academic professionals, 11; faculty architect/program director, 12; faculty involvement, 13–14; institution, 12; internal considerations, 13; mission/vision, 13; students, 12; type/level of degree, 12–13
St. Bonaventure University, 90
strategic plan, 47–48
students, 12, 41; as caretakers, 84; communication, 61; demographics data, 85–86; with disabilities, 82–83; enrollment, 27; FTE enrollments and degrees conferred, 41; projected headcount, 41
student-to-faculty ratio, 91
styles of leadership, 75

target students, 87
target your professional learning, 77
task investigation, 5
teaching or research roles, 73
technology necessary, 87
thrill of leading, 99–100
time, 10
Today's institutions, 44
"to-do" list, 96
trade schools/apprentice programs, 4
traditional faculty, 73
traditional learning methods, 100
type/level of degree, 12–13
types of students, 80–85; adult learners, 81; first-generation students, 82; higher education, 80; immigrant students, 84–85; international students, 83–84; military veterans, 82; part-time students, 83; sex and gender, 80–81; students as caretakers, 84; students with disabilities, 82–83
typical learning outcomes alignment, 60

understanding the place of program: institution, 9; new program, 9; time, 10
University of Minnesota's university, 61
University of Missouri (2024), 63
US Department of Education report, 6

Veterans Administration, 82
vision, 13, 46–47

Wide World of Sports (McKay), 99
willingness to collaborate, 73
write your own story, 102

About the Authors

Gretchen Oltman is an associate professor of interdisciplinary studies at Creighton University in Omaha, Nebraska. She is an attorney, author, university teacher, and leader. She presently leads the Master of Science in Organizational Leadership Program, the Bachelor of Science in Leadership Studies Program, and the Sports Leadership Graduate Certificate Program. Prior to joining Creighton, she worked as the first executive director of the Space, Cyber, and Telecommunications Law LL.M. Program at the University of Nebraska College of Law. She holds a professional Nebraska 7–12 teaching and administrative certificate and spent over a decade working as a high school English teacher. She is the author or coauthor of several education-related titles, including *What's Your Leadership Story? A School Leader's Guide to Aligning How You Lead with Who You Are*, *Prepare to Chair: Leading the Thesis and Dissertation Process*), and *Violence in Student Writing: A Guide for School Administrators*.

Jackie Clark is an associate professor and associate dean in the College of Education and Counseling at Saint Martin's University. She serves as the director for the MEd in Higher Education and Student Affairs Program and as Interim Director for the PhD in leadership studies program. Her research interests include organizational development, college institutional structures, small college environments, institutional leadership, student affairs professional preparation, and assessment practices. As a first-generation student from a working-class family, she is interested in building programs that support students and contribute to their identity as lifelong learners. She holds degrees from the University of Georgia (PhD), Virginia Tech (MA Ed), and Randolph-Macon Woman's College (BA).

www.ingramcontent.com/pod-product-compliance
Lightning Source LLC
Chambersburg PA
CBHW052057230426
43662CB00037B/2011